BOCCONI
UNIVERSITY
PRESS

Stefano Buono
Antonio Ereditato

THE NEW NUCLEAR POWER

A Journey through the Future of Energy

Cover: Cristina Bernasconi, Milano
Illustration: © 2025 Pininfarina S.p.A. (courtesy of)
Typesetting: Valentina Apolloni, Bresso (MI)

Copyright © 2025 Bocconi University Press
EGEA S.p.A.

EGEA S.p.A.
Via Salasco, 5 - 20136 Milano
Tel. 02/5836.5751 – Fax 02/5836.5753
egea.edizioni@unibocconi.it – www.egeaeditore.it

First edition: September 2025

ISBN Domestic Edition   979-12-80623-69-0
ISBN International Edition   979-12-81627-59-8
ISBN Digital International Edition   979-12-81627-73-4
ISBN Epub Edition   979-12-229-8076-8

To Maribel and Paola

Table of Contents

Foreword

For many, nuclear energy is confusing and disturbing, perhaps even more so than fossil fuels, which are the primary cause of air pollution and the source of the climate crisis.

Why? In this book, we will try to provide an answer.

This question is important, because energy is power. Not only political and economic power, but the ability to build things, to make them work and move, and to make life flourish. Access to energy also represents the power to reduce inequalities, and its availability is a form of freedom. This observation is crucial today in view of the stressed international political situation, which is constantly changing, and generates uncertainty and social and economic risks. Serious and far-sighted planning is required, looking well beyond changing contingencies.

Democracy and prosperity for citizens in the next century will depend in part on the degree of energy independence countries are able to develop.

Today, the world is undergoing another of the crucial transitions that throughout human history have involved energy and its supply. Science and technology compelled by the urgency of the climate emergency and the need to 'decarbonise' have leant in and opened new pathways towards sustainability - understood in the broadest sense - prosperity and the well-being of future societies. The ultimate goal is to reduce the impact of human activity on the climate by moving away from fossil fuels to renewable or low-carbon energy sources; 'green' energy, that is, that can address and solve the crisis.

Our world is being constantly enriched by different types of green energy: hydrogen, solar, wind, geothermal, tidal and, above all, by the innovative applications of atomic energy which is neutral from the point of view of greenhouse gas production, and although not 'renewable', is practically eternal. In fact, if used through nuclear fission, the amount of uranium present on the earth's surface would suffice for the planet's energy needs until the natural end of the solar system, in almost five billion years' time.[1] If we add to this the enormous reserve of energy from nuclear fusion, as yet unexploited, we could go much further. Of course, we will unpack this in detail in the pages of this book, for now, we can note that the need to consider the 'new nuclear energy' as one of the tools to bring humanity to decarbonisation was also strongly reiterated at the 2023 UN Climate Change Conference (COP28) in Dubai, where the 198 signatory countries of the UN Framework Convention on Climate Change included nuclear power among the technologies that must be relied upon in the future.

Today we are living through the fourth industrial revolution! The first one at the end of the 18th century was brought about by the invention of the steam engine, the second was caused by the birth of modern industry, and the third initiated by the development of information technology. The fourth now underway and known as 4.0, envisages a world of industry in which many disciplines are exploited horizontally to globally improve productivity and boost consumption and employment. But take note, the fifth industrial revolution, known 5.0 is just around the corner. There is a pressing need for an expansive policy that puts digital - notably artificial intelligence - and green transitions at the centre, in a sustainable eco-system that concentrates on the well-being of all people and our planet. Energy 5.0 is obviously needed for this new revolution.

Indeed, according to data from the World Energy Council's Energy Trilemma Initiative,[2] humanity is already investing more than twice as much in green energy as in fossil fuels ($2 trillion versus $1 trillion), although this basically refers to the economic 'North' of the world: China, Europe and the United States.

For about a hundred years, we have been aware of the enormous energy contained in the atom; this discovery paved the way for the peaceful use of this inexhaustible source with the invention of nuclear reactors. But that is not all. The breakthroughs achieved, with the advent of and revolutionary

---

[1] https://whatisnuclear.com/
[2] https://trilemma.worldenergy.org/

applications in nuclear medicine, and with the increased safety and reliability of nuclear power plants all contribute to defining the nuclear energy of tomorrow, an important component of the green energy portfolio of many countries around the world today, and will be increasingly important in the near future.

The atom can provide us with an energy that offers a clear answer to the need for a decarbonised world and allows us to plan for the future of mankind, including for the most disadvantaged, people, who are currently victims of the choices of the dominant nations. It may seem like a contradiction, but it is precisely nuclear power that has the greatest applications in the field of health care and public health in general: miniaturised batteries for medical exoskeletons and pacemakers, radiation beams for cancer treatment, precision diagnostics and radio-metabolic therapy. But there are also applications in everyday life: mobile phones that recharge every twenty years and micro nuclear reactors to provide low-cost energy for entire districts or large transport ships. And finally, nuclear devices for the space economy.

In our view, the time is ripe to make the perception of the new green and sustainable nuclear power clear, understandable and deliberate. It is the environmentally conscientious choice.

When we met in the early 1990s, as young physicists pursuing their passion and working at CERN (European Council for Nuclear Research), the Geneva laboratory was already a place where scientists from every country came to study, apply innovative ideas and turn them into reality. Built on the ashes of the Second World War, CERN was created precisely to unite scientists from all over the world in the quest for knowledge, for science that was open and peaceful. Perhaps more than other political and economic initiatives, this visionary action by the founding fathers led to building 20th century Europe and giving its citizens a common home. We will come back to this; but while CERN's mission from its inception has been to enable European researchers and their international colleagues to conduct research in the field of fundamental physics, through a range of unique infrastructures, the laboratory has also made it possible to put at the service of the whole of humanity the technological results that have flowed from such research over time, and to apply them to the everyday lives of citizens. Bringing people together under the banner of knowledge, without prejudice, ideology or discrimination, promoting freedom - and not just the freedom of knowledge.

Since those days spent together at CERN, while our personal paths have diverged, our stories, motivations, events, interests and opportunities have intertwined and chased each other, under the umbrella of curiosity and the desire to explore new paths: research, academia, entrepreneurship, and also the dissemination of our work, to allow as many people as possible to participate in the fantastic game of basic scientific research and its amazing applications. Today we meet here again, with the desire to establish a special, sincere and mature relationship with the reader, without manipulation, talking about a new model for the development of society, one that places energy and its sustainability at the centre, precisely because of its nature as an instrument capable of changing the destiny of humanity.

In thirty years, many things have changed, in the world as a whole and also in science and technology. Progress has moved fast, and continues to do so, with exponential changes. Yesterday's discovery becomes today's application and tomorrow's routine procedures. The atomic nucleus and its energy is no exception. This book is a necessary opportunity to make everyone a little more aware of scientific progress and in this way to contribute, finally, to making intelligent, strategic and future thinking justified choices based on the science. The aim is to place science at the centre of the debate, especially because science is currently under attack in various areas, in a totally unjustified manner.

In the field of energy needs and supply, it is not necessary to use a sledgehammer, but to work carefully, intelligently, adapting needs and proposals as best as we can, avoiding wrong or crude choices, and putting needs, security, efficiency, health, sustainability and economics at the forefront, through 'balanced energy portfolios', just as is done with financial investments. We must plan energy choices today to define the social, economic and technological development of tomorrow, without improvising or jumping on the bandwagon of contingency, or senseless knee jerk panic and group think as exemplified by approaches such as: "Gas costs too much? Then let's burn coal!", "Petrol is not green; only electric cars!", or "Nuclear power plants can be bombed; let's turn them off!".

Fortunately, the galloping scientific and technological development that characterises our age produces ever new solutions, powerful tools even for the 5.0 energy race of the future. While the human being must always be placed at the centre of any reasonable development plan, it would be folly to turn away and not listen to the powerful indications that science and technology give us.

The book has been structured as an exploratory and informative journey by using a literal map through the places of energy. We chose these destinations precisely because, and to highlight the issues of energy and its supply are in the limelight as never before.

Since we are Italian, we sometimes refer to specific examples concerning our country, but we believe that many of our observations have a sufficiently universal character. Our ambition is to make a small contribution to an essential conversation that is internationally relevant, no matter where you live. We intend to be clear and accessible. Of course, we will also touch on what we have most recently learnt and achieved in the field of new-generation nuclear energy, a topic that is very dear to us, in order to use explanations and facts to contribute to producing a new awareness on the macro-theme of energy.

We have decided to close the book with our 'dream' of a near future in which science and technology will be even more central humankind's ally in every respect, not instruments of control and standardisation in a dystopian world, but perhaps generators of a new stable and shared humanism.

1 On an Oil Platform, in the Gulf of Mexico

Energy Sources and Global Warming

Even from a distance, the visual impact is remarkable. The helicopter approaches rapidly, allowing us to observe more and more details of the imposing structure that seems to emerge from the water, above the waves. An intricate complex of two hundred thousand tonnes of pipes, beams and heavy mechanical devices, as tall as a six-storey building, resting on gigantic piles and capable of withstanding earthquakes of magnitude 9 on the Richter scale. Its job is to extract from the bowels of the earth, from even more than a kilometre below the relatively shallow Caribbean seabed, what decades ago was called black gold, loved and sought after by all. Today, on the one hand, it is an outcast considered responsible for all the ills of the planet, and on the other, still an indispensable player in the consumer society, always in search of more energy for its needs.

Humanity is indeed terribly energy-hungry: in one year, we consume as much energy as the Sun produces in one hour of operation. Put this way, it does not sound like an impressive amount, but this is deceiving. Like all other stars, the Sun is a highly efficient (and gigantic) nuclear fusion reactor. For about five million millennia, every second it has been constantly and steadily consuming 600 million tonnes of hydrogen - the essential element in its composition - converting it into 596 million tonnes of helium. The missing 4 million tonnes are transformed into an immense amount of energy, thanks to the equivalence between mass and energy, described by Einstein's famous equation: $E = mc^2$. Nevertheless, despite these extraordinary numbers, the Sun is only halfway through its long life. And almost all forms of energy that we encounter on our planet are directly or indirectly generated by the Sun, coming from the infinite transformations to which energy is continuously subjected.

The huge platform cost over a billion dollars and several years of work to build. As many as one hundred thousand barrels per day are extracted, whereas a normal surface oil well produces a few hundred at most. More than two hundred people work on the enterprise, all highly specialised and well-paid technicians, given the working conditions which are at best unusual, if not prohibitive, with long periods spent on this large infrastructure in the middle of the ocean, accompanied only by their colleagues, soldiers in a technological Tartar Desert. Workers are mechanical and electronic experts, but also cooks and doctors. Like all large industrial plants in heavy industry and energy supply, the platform operates continuously, 24/7. These numbers give us an idea of the value of the oil the rig extracts over its long lifetime.

Finding oil, before extracting it, requires careful search work. First, geologists and geophysicists have to identify the existence of potential deposits. It is estimated that at least fifty billion tonnes of black gold are hidden under the seabed, down to depths of several kilometres. Exploration is reminiscent of the search for water by the roots of a tree: thanks to powerful steel drills covered with extremely hard artificial diamonds, the underwater rock is progressively pierced until mechanical roots locate the deposit: large pockets containing oil, or in other cases, large spaces filled with natural gas. The black liquid is at very high pressure, placing stringent demands on the safety of the structure and its inhabitants. An incorrect extraction procedure could easily lead to disaster - let us recall, for example, the Deepwater Horizon rig accident, which in 2010, in this very area, caused the death of eleven workers and the spillage of more than five million barrels of oil into the sea, not to mention the more than five hundred million dollars lost in the destruction of the infrastructure. But today's technology is very advanced, fortunately. There are redundant safety systems, and most processes are automated and assisted by numerous computers and monitoring devices.

Freshly extracted oil appears as a thick, unattractive liquid, dark and sticky like tar. It can be temporarily stored in huge concrete caissons below sea level or, as is the case here in the Gulf of Mexico, immediately fed into an intricate network of underwater pipelines connected to coastal infrastructures, which manage the next steps of handling, purification and logistics. It all sounds perfect. An effective mechanism to 'harvest' the fruit that nature has graciously bestowed upon us for our needs, to meet the great hunger for energy that we have developed, exponentially, over the last two hundred years. But we now know that the optimism of the last century is misplaced. If not properly addressed, this only apparently virtuous mechanism of collecting and using fossil fuels, such as oil, natural gas and coal, will lead us to ruin. Not to that of the planet, which since its birth has always been strong and resilient, but to that of our arrogant species, probably wrongly called Sapiens. Other forms of life will survive, which will be able to adapt Darwinianly to the terrible conditions that lie ahead if the proclaimed climate crisis is not resolved, very soon.

In this regard, a few hundred kilometres from this platform, on what is now the Yucatan Peninsula, on an unknown day, of an unknown year, of an undefined millennium some 66 million years ago, an epoch-making event occurred. An enormous asteroid, which certainly exceeded ten kilometres in diameter, appeared ominously in the sky, followed by a sinister trail of fire and accompanied by a deafening hissing sound. It thunderously entered the warm waters of the Gulf of Mexico at an angle of about fifty degrees to vertical, generating on impact a crater nearly two hundred kilometres in diameter and over twenty deep. The energy dissipated in the impact was immense, at least equal to that of several tens of millions of atomic bombs. Instantaneously, a shocking tsunami was generated, several hundred metres high, which quickly propagated for hundreds of kilometres, destroying all plant and animal life in its path. Ashes, vapours and incandescent fragments were emitted at high speed in all directions, falling back to the ground and generating secondary damage over extensive territories through vast fires. The shockwave of the blast propagated very quickly, triggering a series of collateral events, earthquakes in particular. Many unsuspecting animals died instantly as in a gigantic Pompeii, but the worst was yet to come. Immense amounts of dust and ash scattered throughout the planet's atmosphere and remained suspended for many years, creating an unprecedented greenhouse effect; acid rain and substantial climate change. The sudden blanket of dust prevented the arrival of sunlight for a long time, significantly cooling the planet's surface and killing most of the green plants.

Eventually, almost all living beings paid the price: over 70 per cent of the animal and plant species on Earth became extinct in short order. Among them were the non-avian dinosaurs, undisputed lords and masters of the Earth's ecosystems for over 160 million years. Along with them, the various living species that were symbiotically close to the dinosaurs disappeared. Fortunately, we were not there. On the contrary, the event was selfishly beneficial, such that millions of years later, human beings could appear. In fact, among the species that survived and managed to overcome the global crisis were our distant ancestors, the first small mammals. In that case, a long, cold winter produced a mass extinction. Today, it may be the opposite: the anomalous, anthropogenic warming of the planet may produce equally severe effects. But we do not have a plan B; we must make it, and eventually we will make it, thanks to the great opportunity that the meteorite from long ago has given us, to continue towards a future that has not yet been written. And the new energy will be the key to our success.

The cause of the problem

The starting point for understanding man-made global warming is energy. Fossil fuels - oil, coal and natural gas - originated from biomass deposited in prehistoric eras and then accumulated underground. They were created by energy from the Sun, as are wind power, hydroelectric power, and tidal power, all generated in the sequential transformation of energy sources from solar radiant energy. The direct radiation of our star, however, is partially reflected outwards - about 30 per cent - by the outer layers of the atmosphere or even by clouds. What manages to penetrate is partly absorbed by the planet's surface and all living organisms, while a small fraction is reflected back into space. Apart from variations that can be well explained by the slow progress of solar or terrestrial events, the system consisting of the Earth and its atmosphere has been able to regulate itself effectively for millions of years through the absorption and reflection of the Sun's heat, thus determining the optimal conditions for biological life on the Earth, which has adapted Darwinianly to these very conditions over millions of years. In fact, without this 'natural greenhouse effect', the planet's average surface temperature would be about –20°C instead of about +15 today, making the Earth completely inhospitable.

The main actor in the energy-climate interaction is the production/absorption mechanism involving carbon dioxide (whose chemical formula is CO_2) and oxygen, caused by the synergy between animal species - consumers of oxygen and generators of CO_2 - and plant species - de facto users of CO_2 and producers of oxygen. Thanks to this dynamic process, which is very sensitive to external, geological or astrophysical events, both the temperature and the concentration of carbon dioxide have varied cyclically over the millions of years of the planet's recent life but never has so much been happening since man began the extensive exploitation of the Earth's natural and fossil energy resources. Let us consider that in the last few hundred thousand years, the percentage of CO_2 in the atmosphere has fluctuated around an average value of about 230 parts per million; since the beginning of the industrial age, with the massive combustion of oil, gas and coal, this value has started to increase unceasingly, reaching about 420 parts per million today; an increase that cannot quantitatively be interpreted as due to natural causes (whether astronomical or geophysical).

In combustion, fossil substances are chemically transformed by generating heat. Among such compounds, coal and hydrocarbons produced from oil (gases and liquids) play a special role today. The basic ingredients are a substance rich in carbon (the chemical symbol is C) and oxygen (symbol O). Two oxygen atoms combine to form a gaseous oxygen molecule (O_2) that is found abundantly in the earth's atmosphere, allowing life to exist on the planet. Suppose then that we have methane (whose formula is CH_4, indicating the bond between a carbon atom and four hydrogen atoms, H). In the presence of oxygen and an initial source of energy - *e.g.* the heat of an ignition flame, such as that of a cigarette lighter - the reaction $CH_4 + 2O_2$ $CO_2 + 2H_2O$ + energy takes place, the latter being in the form of heat. The formula reads as follows (Figure 1): One molecule of methane reacts chemically with two molecules of oxygen, which together with heat produce 'waste' products: one molecule of carbon dioxide (CO_2) and two molecules of water (H_2O). This reaction continues as long as there is sufficient oxygen and methane, producing much more heat energy than the little needed for ignition. This allows us to make an observation that will be useful later on: when assuming a form of energy, we must always be certain that we consume less energy to activate it than we then obtain! It sounds trivial, but when speaking of energy costs, this is obviously something to take into account.

Figure 1 Release of energy and CO_2 from the combustion of a hydrocarbon

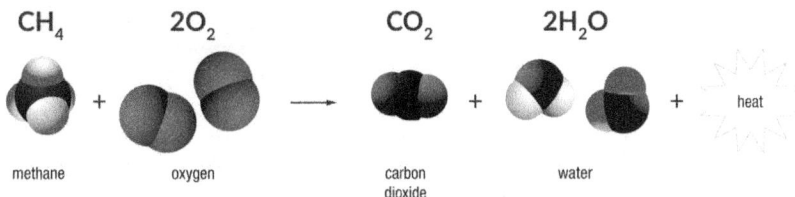

CH_4	$2O_2$	CO_2	$2H_2O$	
methane	oxygen	carbon dioxide	water	heat

The correlation between the human-generated increase in CO_2 and other greenhouse gases, on the one hand, and the rise in the planet's average temperature, on the other, has been incontrovertibly scientifically proven (Figure 2), thanks in part to the scientific reports produced since 1990 by the Intergovernmental Panel on Climate Change (IPCC)[1] established by the United Nations. Global warming is the phenomenon that highlights the change in the Earth's climate that has taken place over the last two centuries - truly an instant in comparison to the long history of the planet and its flora and fauna. The most characteristic aspect of the crisis is that even a small increase in the concentration of particular gases in the atmosphere, such as CO_2 or methane, reduces the fraction of energy re-radiated from the Earth to outer space, generating a process similar to what happens in greenhouses for agriculture. In fact, since the Earth itself emits radiant energy, but at much longer wavelengths than the Sun

Figure 2 Increase in global mean temperatures as a function of time since 1940

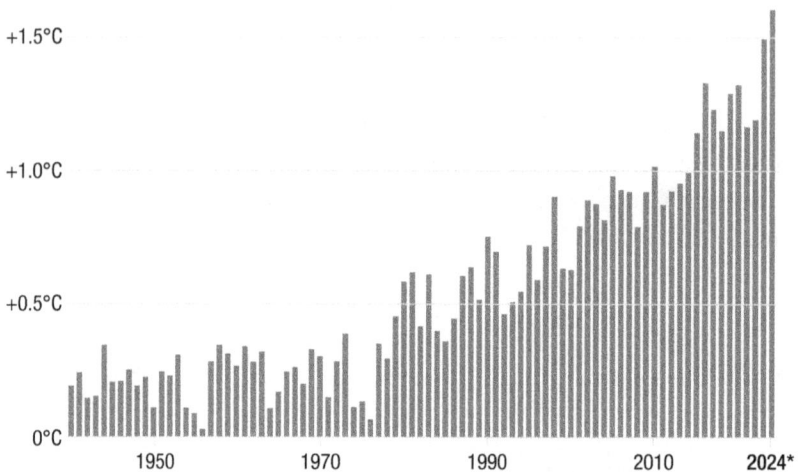

* Provisional estimate for 2024 based on 10 months (January to October)

Source: Copernicus Climate Change Service/ECMWF (https://climate.copernicus.eu/copernicus-2024-virtually-certain-be-warmest-year-and-first-year-above-15degc).

[1] https://www.ipcc.ch/

- because it is much colder - part of this long-wave radiation is absorbed by the greenhouse gases, which re-transmit this energy in all directions, including downwards, thus trapping heat in the atmosphere. As a result of the enormous amounts of solar energy trapped in the Earth's delicate ecological system, the average temperature of the planet rises. The result is a significant rise in the Earth's temperature that is still ongoing and that requires us all to be committed to finding a solution to the problem, for the sake of the planet and future generations.

One might assume that the increase of two or three degrees in the planet's temperature compared to the historical average is after all a small thing - a typical argument of the deniers. This is not the case at all. Just think of a large pot full of water: in order to raise its temperature by a few degrees or, at the very least, bring the water to a boil, it is necessary to keep it on the fire for a very long time, thus administering a considerable amount of energy to it; technically, it is said that the water in the pot possesses a large heat capacity. This physical variable is of enormous value to the Earth's ecosystem, which is why an increase of just a few degrees is matched by an immense additional amount of solar energy released into the atmosphere, which in turn is capable of generating an abnormal number of what are called extreme weather events: floods, droughts, fires, hurricanes, typhoons, heat waves. Yet that is not all; there are also indirect effects. Think of the accumulation of CO_2 in the oceans. This gas causes irreversible damage to phytoplankton, which produces about 50 per cent of the planet's oxygen. Or think of the albedo effect, which is the reflective power of a terrestrial surface to outer space: snow and ice, especially concentrated in the Arctic and Antarctic regions, have a high albedo and much of the sunlight that hits icy surfaces bounces back. In contrast, dark surfaces have a low albedo and therefore absorb more sunlight. Therefore, snow and ice that are covered in soot from pollution no longer reflect sunlight, but instead absorb it, causing an increase in their melting. This process is also strongly dependent on global warming, meaning that if glaciers continue to melt, more energy will be retained in the atmosphere, increasing the temperature even more, leading to a vicious circle.

What are the details of global greenhouse gas production? More than 70 per cent comes from the use of energy for civil or industrial purposes (about 30 billion tonnes of CO_2 produced in 2020 alone[2]). Industry con-

---

[2] https://ourworldindata.org/ghg-emissions-by-sector

tributes about 30 per cent (mainly cement, steel and chemical production) and transport 15 per cent. This implies that direct emissions - industry and transport - are not only dominant, but unfortunately also relatively incompressible, at least in the short and medium term. Science and technology can certainly come to our aid, and we must have confidence in this process: we can increase energy efficiency, use new sources such as hydrogen[3] or solar energy, and disseminate CO_2 capture and storage methods on a large scale. It is also important to note that - contrary to a simplistic narrative - developing countries are certainly not the main ones responsible for this waste. In 2023, China produced approximately 8.4 tonnes of CO_2 per inhabitant, India 2.1 tonnes and the USA as much as 14.3 tonnes per US citizen (Figure 3). The wealthiest populations contribute to these figures, and thus their well-being costs the rest of humanity a great deal in terms of environmental impact. This places a duty on the more developed countries to implement and propose sustainable solutions for the energy of the future, also by virtue of their scientific-technological knowledge. Furthermore, the Carbon Majors report for 2023[4] indicates that about half of the world's CO_2 production comes from a group of only twenty to thirty companies, both private and state-owned.

In any case, removing excess CO_2 from the atmosphere seems like a dream, hardly feasible at the moment: between now and 2100, we would have to eliminate or store some 15 billion tonnes of greenhouse gases per year. Capturing and storing CO_2 from the atmosphere is also a technically complex procedure, although it is not something completely new. It can be achieved, for example, by containing the gas in construction cement, after extraction from the air, or by reacting it with appropriate rocks at great depths.

From a cultural and social point of view, a Copernican revolution is necessary, to supplant once and for all the anthropocentrism and selfishness of individuals in favour of a more rational, i.e. broader and less naïve, view of the world. Our globe should be understood pragmatically as a small planet in the immense universe, in which only a great stroke of luck

---

[3] To be precise, we will then see that hydrogen is not really a source of energy, but a means of storing and transporting it.
[4] https://carbonmajors.org/briefing/The-Carbon-Majors-Database-2023-Update-31397

Figure 3   Average CO_2 emissions per capita per country, calculated as total emissions
divided by population. Excluding international transport

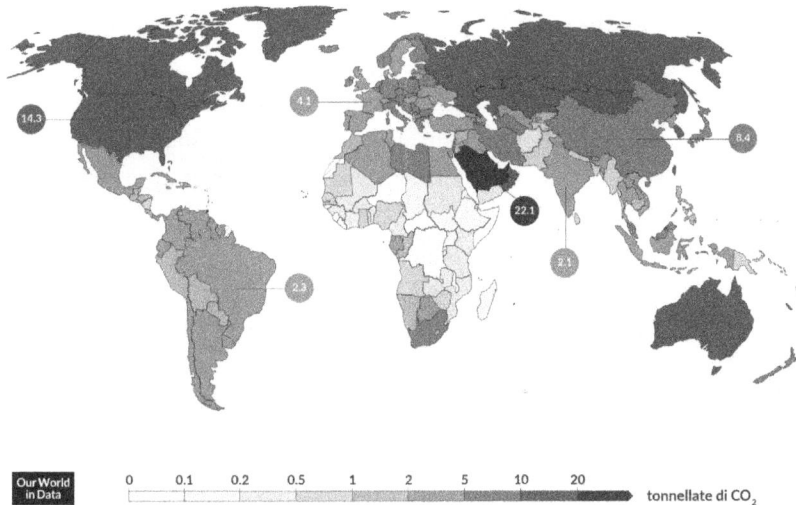

Source: *Our World in Data* (https://ourworldindata.org/grapher/co-emissions-per-capita?tab=map).

made our birth and evolution as a living species possible. A good reason to keep it clean and tidy!

The solution to the problem

The basic question is whether there are viable alternatives to the use of fossil fuels. The answer is yes. Take the example of electricity that is rightly considered green: cars with combustion engines may be banned in the not-too-distant future in favour of their electric sisters, although this transition, which started with a surge a few years ago, seems to be slowing down. Even bicycles are electrified, and taking the train instead of the plane is considered a sign of respect and love for nature. But is electricity really a special source of energy? As with other energy sources, it can be produced by converting or transforming other forms of energy (green and otherwise!). Consider, for example, electric batteries. Thanks to the energy generated by appropriate chemical reactions, positive and negative electrical charges are separated, creating a potential difference in the device. In a different way, the energy from the Sun's light activates physical reactions in photovoltaic cells, which are electrical devices made of silicon; when sunlight strikes the surface of the cells, it can generate an electric current (energy). Alternatively, when suitably concentrated by converging mirrors, sunlight can be used directly to heat gases, liquids or solids and produce heat (again, energy), potentially generating high-temperature steam with which to run turbines to produce electricity.

This latter process is the most significant system for generating electricity, one based on the principles of electromagnetism. We know that an electric current created by a potential difference produces a magnetic field. Symmetrically, a variable magnetic field creates an electric current. This is what normally happens in the dynamo of a bicycle or the turbine of a hydroelectric power station. The difference lies in the starting energy that is converted into electricity: in the first case, the 'biological' energy of the cyclist's muscles, and in the second case, the 'potential' energy due to the gradient of the waterfall. And we could go on and on: the wind can turn wind turbines, and these drive an electric turbine, and the force of the tides can operate turbines immersed in the moving sea stream.

In other very common cases, however, electricity is also generated by driving turbines using thermal engines that run on gas, coal or diesel, such as auxiliary generators or industrial electricity generators. It is obvious that in this case we have produced electricity, but using non-renewable energy, which is responsible for the climate crisis. It should be remembered that by *renewable* we mean those forms of energy that, once used, are restored to nature within a time compatible with the human lifespan, without having to wait millennia or millions of years. We are therefore thinking of energy from the Sun, the tides, geothermal or wind power, and so on, and certainly not energy from fossil fuels such as coal and oil, which take millions of years to be produced, and thus to be restored to nature, and which may possibly be exhausted within a few generations. As we shall see, nuclear energy is also non-renewable, but it is climate-neutral and therefore to be considered green for all intents and purposes. We thus understand that the main characteristics of the energy of the future are not only its 'renewability', but its ability not to generate greenhouse gases, its low cost, and its sustainable integration into an ever-changing social context.

We now leave the large oil platform, departing by helicopter, the only means capable of connecting its resident community to the mainland. The life of the station will still be long. It will realistically continue to extract oil for decades, which will contribute more CO_2 to the atmosphere.

The use of fossil fuels is reminiscent of the issue of tobacco consumption: the manufacturers make profits, states collect money from taxes on cigarettes, yet everyone knows that smoking is seriously harmful to health and advises against its use. But decarbonisation will have to come, despite everything. Global warming, 'thankfully', has in recent years become an increasingly important factor when discussing energy supply and has finally entered public opinion, and hopefully, the agendas of policy-makers in an overbearing - and lasting - way.

The helicopter quickly takes us to a nearby airport, from where we embark on a short flight to a small town in the southern United States. There we will begin to address the question of how, practically speaking, energy can be derived from the nucleus of the atom in a peaceful and environmentally friendly manner.

2 At a Nuclear Power Plant in the Southwest US

Without Prejudice

As soon as we enter, we find ourselves together with groups of visitors, consisting of school groups and private citizens, curious to see a nuclear reactor up close and understand how it works. Immediately after the entrance, a large room houses a refreshment area, where visitors mingle with employees, all focused on sandwiches and drinks, waiting to get back to work or leave for the guided tour. We join the latter. The guide explains that work on the construction of the large power station began in the early 1970s. It took ten years for it to start operating - the typical time to build even a large modern-day plant - transforming the heat from the fission reactions in the core of the two reactors into electricity. The plant, we are told, will operate as it is until at least 2040. It is a so-called second-generation facility: that is, one of the first to be used for the continuous production of electricity.

Walking along long corridors crammed with pipes and electromechanical devices, we pass through a number of rooms housing the various mechanical and electrical workshops, where skilled workers seem calmly intent on routine work. It is all very relaxed, without the tension one would imagine for an activity related to nuclear reactions and power generation. The plant rather resembles a heavy industry, routinely engaged in producing some kind of complex artefacts. In some ways, it is like being at CERN, in one of the many laboratories supporting research activities. Here, too, we see the various radiation control and screening devices typical of large research institutes or hospitals where radiation is used for medical purposes. These are particle and electromagnetic radiation detectors, the 'application offspring' of the detectors designed, built and used in centres such as CERN to conduct physics experiments; an excellent example of technology transfer.

We approach the heart of the plant: the twin reactors are in full operation. Each of the two consists of a core of about two hundred units, each containing many uranium-based fissile fuel rods, immersed in a large pool of water, used as a 'moderator' for the fission reactions and for cooling the reactor. Another water circuit, strictly separated from the first, transports the heat released in the nuclear reactions to the steam turbines, which produce electricity from the driving force of high-pressure water vapour. The pipes prosaically resemble those in the heating apparatus of a large building. Pumps and servomechanisms have little science fiction about them, and the turbines themselves look no different from those of a hydroelectric, gas or coal-fired power plant. The turbines generate high-voltage electricity (around 200,000 volts) which, thanks to large transformers, is increased to 500,000 volts before being fed into the transmission and distribution network. Power losses along the transport pathway with electric pylons are reduced as the voltage increases. Just think that the power station supplies the energy needed by more than 650,000 households.

We then enter the brain of the infrastructure: the control room. Here, too, a soporific silence reigns. A few technicians, responsible for monitoring the various types of equipment, do more or less the work a physicists at CERN during their shifts in the control rooms - the researchers' long eight-hour moves consist of watching monitors, running test programmes and being alert to possible alarms, caused by the malfunction of some device. All is quiet, including the gentle jazz music coming from a small speaker used by one of the operators. They point out that all the security and control systems are oversized and redundant, along the lines of what happens in aircraft. The warning lights, now all green, number more than a thousand, although most of them would only indicate the trivial failure of a fan or an accessory pump. The technicians in charge of the shifts are skilled and trained, including through courses conducted on simulators, just like aircraft pilots.

Passive systems are added to these active protections. The hearts of the two reactors are protected by various structures and shields of concrete and steel with an onion skin structure, capable of withstanding earthquakes, plane crashes, deliberate acts and... human error. The history of Chernobyl has taught us that it makes little sense to talk about computer or servomechanism malfunctions, whereas human operators must be more careful. This is why checklists, double or triple checks and shared actions between several people make the operation of the infrastructure safe and efficient. Of this, the droves of schoolchildren intent on listening to the guides explaining the secrets of the power plant seem very aware and empowered.

Atomic nuclei, cells and DNA

A common diagnostic examination is magnetic resonance imaging (MRI), which is very useful in many medical fields as it allows for non-invasive observation of the body's internal tissues to identify any abnormalities or lesions. The full name of the instrument is 'nuclear magnetic resonance'; nothing to do with atomic radiation, but doctors - and perhaps even the sellers of the devices - prefer not to use the full and correct wording so as to avoid misunderstandings or objections from patients. At most, they use the harmless acronym MRI. We will return to this very important topic later: as mentioned above, there is a very close link between the results of research in nuclear physics and medicine, through diagnostics and therapy.

Similarly, when discussing possible energy sources and requirements to meet our society's needs, sooner or later 'nuclear' is mentioned, meaning 'the energy derived from the atomic nucleus'. And it often happens that from a psychological point of view, radiation is seen as a silent and devious enemy, capable of producing enormous damage without even being evident. After all, who has ever seen a proton or a beta ray? However, the aversion and instinctive fear towards nuclear energy often manifests itself in a contradictory manner. Who among us would not agree to undergo anti-cancer radiation therapy, a diagnostic PET scan, a mammogram or a simple X-ray at a dentist? In this case, radiation - sometimes administered in considerable doses - is certainly welcome, as we have confidence in the promised (or hoped-for) results.

Be that as it may, it is true that the three types of radiation generated by the particular elements known as radioactive elements - alpha, beta and gamma radiation (we will see their characteristics in Chapter 3) - can interact with biological tissues and cause damage. This is generally referred to as ionising radiation, as it is capable of stripping electrons from atoms and molecules, thus changing their chemical structure. At high energies, such radiation can also penetrate atomic nuclei, producing reactions of a nuclear nature - nucleus fission is an example of this, which we will discuss in the next chapter from the standpoint of its physical principles.

The biological effects of radiation emitted by radioactive substances are well known. Ionising radiation, in particular, can affect cells by altering their genetic material, breaking or otherwise damaging cellular

DNA. Such alterations can cause mutations and these, in turn, cause cancerous lesions; if the damage is too severe, in the case of high amounts of radiation, the affected cells can even die. Fortunately, cells are generally able to repair DNA damage, provided that they have not been 'too badly damaged' or that these repair mechanisms are unable to function properly for other biological reasons. In addition to the size of the dose,[1] it is important to consider the synergy of radiation with other biological or genetic risk factors. Indeed, some genetically predisposed individuals may be hypersensitive to even small doses of radiation. But, above all, when discussing phenomena such as radioactivity, one must be quantitative. We should not forget, in fact, that for as long as life has existed on our planet we have been continuously bombarded by what is called *cosmic radiation*, which varies in type and intensity depending on altitude. At sea level it corresponds to a flux of about one electrically charged particle per square centimetre per minute through our bodies. Not to mention the ultraviolet photons from the Sun or the radiation generated by the substances and materials of our daily lives: concrete or tuff walls or chemicals. We even ingest radioactive potassium from bananas! At this point, we are led to consider that this unavoidable phenomenon, called 'background' radiation, has actually contributed positively to our evolution, producing a continuous rate of genetic mutations that, in the long run, may have been beneficial to our Darwinian adaptation to the environment.

Radiation generates two types of effects on biological tissues: *deterministic* and *probabilistic* (stochastic). The former become apparent after exposure, but only when the intensity of the radiation exceeds a certain threshold dose that depends on the particular organ or tissue. Above that threshold, of course, the higher the dose, the more serious the problems. Probabilistic effects, on the other hand, can occur even a long time after exposure, and the higher the dose, the greater the likelihood that they will actually occur one day. Since DNA alterations can be transferred to subsequent generations of cells, this can lead, as mentioned, to malignant lesions.

It should also be noted that the three types of radiation interact differently with our bodies. Alpha radiation, for example, is not very pene-

---

[1] The physical quantity of 'dose' defines the energy absorbed by an object per unit mass (*e.g.* an organ of the human body) when exposed to radiation.

trating and can only cause damage to the eyes, or to the lungs if for some reason it affects the inner mucous membrane (think of radon gas, which emits such radiation and can be inhaled). Beta electrons and high-energy gamma photons, on the other hand, are relatively penetrating and can also damage internal tissues. Finally, we must not forget the potentially serious effects of interaction with biological tissues by energy particles such as protons and neutrons, generated in various physical processes, and specifically, in the explosion of nuclear devices, or that are present in space, no longer shielded by the atmosphere.

In order to have the necessary quantitative perception of the problem, it is good to introduce the unit of measurement of the quantity used to assess the biological effect of radiation absorption by living organisms, the *millisievert* (mSv). Without going into technical details, let us note that the aforementioned (ineliminable) background radiation - which, by the way, depends on how radioactive the environments or geographical locations in which we find ourselves are - corresponds to 1-5 mSv per year. For comparison, a chest X-ray is 1.5 mSv and a CT scan of the lungs is 8 mSv, but these are absorbed in one shot and concentrated in one part of the body. For the sake of completeness, the lethal dose for a human being is 5,000 mSv distributed over the entire body. This value is not very different from that corresponding to a two-year round trip to Mars: such a mission would provide the heroic astronauts with a total of 800 mSv, making the probability of serious genetic damage a virtual certainty. We must not forget, however, that the blade of a knife that kills in one context, can also cut through a tumour in the operating theatre. The metaphor is apt. As we shall see later, the mechanisms of cell damage by radiation also apply (all the more so!) to cancer cells.

Another interesting example concerns cigarette smoking. Everyone knows that the incidence of lung cancer among smokers is more than twenty times higher than it is among non-smokers, and that 90 per cent of these diseases are smoking-related, leading to the dramatic level of two million deaths per year worldwide. A fraction of these pathologies, however, are not due to the carcinogenic power of nicotine or tar: given the use of fertilisers - which contain radioactive substances - cigarette tobacco retains part of these elements which are emitters of alpha radiation (notably polonium); these release all their energy with the matter placed in direct contact with the source. Smoke carries this radiation to the inner surface of the lungs, adding its damage to that of nicotine and other chemicals, including tar, carbon monoxide, formaldehyde, benzene, acetone, toluene, ammonia and other toxic and carcinogenic compounds. It is estimated that smoking a packet of cigarettes a day for a year is equivalent to undergoing more than thirty chest X-rays!

Two important lessons

What happened on 26 April 1986 at the Chernobyl power plant in Ukraine was a largely unexpected event that has remained in history, contributing to the perceived danger associated with nuclear energy. As a result of the plant's unsafe design (lack of a containment building) and avoidable human error, due to an unnecessary technical exercise,[2] the tank of one of the reactors exploded - with a conventional, and certainly not nuclear, deflagration - and the graphite control rods caught fire, projecting a considerable amount of radioactive material to an altitude of many kilometres, for several days. The dispersion of the dust contaminated the neighbouring regions of southern Belarus, northern Ukraine and the bordering regions of Russia. On the morning of the accident, some 600 workers were present at the plant. Of these, 134 received high doses and quickly developed very serious illnesses: 28 died within three months, while another 19 perished between 1987 and 2004 from illnesses that could not be attributed with certainty to radiation exposure, due to the random nature of biological radiation damage. The others more or less recovered over some time. Despite the seriousness of the incident, the immediate number of human casualties was undoubtedly very small for an event of this magnitude.

Although the episode should by no means be minimised or dismissed - not least because of the consequent pollution of the environment, the large clean-up costs and the considerable social problems - it is important

---

[2] Franco Casali, a professor of nuclear reactor physics, effectively summarised the main reason for the accident: 'Imagine a mammoth aircraft with 16 engines and a thousand passengers on board. Imagine also that the pilot [or rather, both pilots in agreement with each other -ed.] at a certain point, in the grip of a rapture, starts doing manoeuvres as if he were in command of a small aerobatic show jet and that, wanting to outdo himself, *he does a loop* with the inevitable consequence of crashing to the ground. I am sure you will say: that was not a plane crash but an act of madness. That is what happened at Chernobyl'.

that the primary discourse on the damage caused to the population be rigorous. In 2008, a report was produced on behalf of the United Nations by the United Nations Scientific Committee on the Effects of Atomic Radiation, with the aim of quantifying the medical and biological effects over medium and long periods of time. Here too, the numbers are in stark contrast to the popular narrative and the various fake news stories that have been circulating on the subject over the years: deformed animals, slaughter of children and abnormal abortions. On the other hand, there were around 6,000 additional cases of thyroid cancer among the residents of Belarus, the Russian Federation and Ukraine from 1986 to 2005 among children and adolescents exposed at the time of the accident, a disease that could largely have been avoided by quickly administering iodine pills, but which did not, however, lead to a similar number of deaths. By the end of 2016, the number of cancer cases had risen to 11,000. Undoubtedly, a proportion of the diagnoses can be attributed to the implementation of screening programmes following the disaster, although most can be reasonably attributed to radiation exposure in the immediate aftermath.

According to the report, though, apart from the issue of thyroid cancer, there is no evidence of a further impact on public health attributable to radiation exposure, even forty years later. There is no scientific evidence of increases in mortality rates, nor of growth in the incidence of non-neoplastic diseases that can be correlated with the event. In the eighty years since that day in 1986, the total number of deaths from cancer is estimated at about 4,000, which compares with the much larger number of about one million people who die in a single year from other forms of cancer. By comparison: normal pollution due to the use of fossil fuels causes over one to two million deaths per year (depending on the estimate) from various diseases attributed - this time with certainty - to these energy sources. The disproportion is extremely significant. Incidentally, over three million people around the world are cured of cancer each year by radiation used in medical therapies.

The total number of human casualties due to accidents at nuclear power plants - to date the only victims have been at Chernobyl - gives us a quantitative and objective measure of the risk associated with such infrastructure. We are in an even better situation than the risk of air travel. Air transport is certainly safer than car transport or even cycling, given the fatal accidents they cause: over 1.3 million deaths a year worldwide from car accidents, compared to a couple of hundred victims from plane crashes (a number which varies greatly in time). Clearly, these numbers must be correctly normalised to the number of travellers by one or the other means of transport and the kilometres travelled, but even then, air transport is still the safest. The problem is that the rare catastrophes in the skies immediately leap to the public's eye and are generally very visible, just like anomalies and (very rare) accidents at nuclear power plants. On the other hand, other energy sources, fossil fuels first of all, have over the last two centuries caused a large number of serious accidents and a great many lives lost; in this case, though, the results soon passed into oblivion because they are less sensationalised and 'newsworthy' than Chernobyl or Fukushima. Not counting the aforementioned one to two million deaths per year due to fossil fuel pollution,[3] we have had over one hundred thousand deaths due to mining accidents in America alone, in addition to oil tanker accidents that have polluted the coastlines of many countries with enormous ecological damage, and the many explosions in conventional power plants all over the world.

However, the concrete goal is for future 'fourth generation' fission reactors, which are currently being designed and authorised, to enjoy safety and reliability standards that are even higher than those of the previous generation operating today; we speak here of *intrinsic safety*, *i.e.* the absence of risk of a destructive accident. Likewise, the high degree of infrastructure automation will effectively eliminate the risk of reckless human actions similar to those at Chernobyl. And yet, despite these numbers and statistics, the use of nuclear energy has been the subject of decisions dictated by political and social arguments on the part of various countries, due to emotional or ideological issues, but also to technical and objective ones: the disposal of radioactive waste generated by the 'spent' fuel, the great cost and time involved in setting up energy production plants, the requirement for continuous availability of cooling with water from nearby rivers or lakes, passive safety issues against deliberate human attacks, aeroplane crashes and the like.

However, nuclear power, like the general topic of energy supply, is primarily a cultural issue and therefore specific to each country. And the nuclear power of today, as well as that of tomorrow, will be able to meet

---

[3] https://ourworldindata.org/safest-sources-of-energy

society's needs thanks in part to the great scientific and technological progress that has been made in recent decades. That is not all: if forty years ago we could afford to renounce such an economically viable source of energy supply on the basis of political and ideological choices, relying on a greater contribution from fossil fuels, today the climate crisis and the various international tensions existing no longer allow us to cling to short-sighted or emotional options that postpone the solution of problems to future generations, especially with regard to the economy and energy independence.

The situation is emblematically similar to that of modern waste-to-energy plants. Active in all the world's major cities, they solve waste management in a much safer, more ecological and reliable manner than landfills, and even create economic benefits thanks to the ancillary production of energy and substances that can be used by industry. In Italy, however, we are still witnessing incomprehensible objections that are completely unjustified and strongly ideological. In the meantime, our waste accumulates in landfills - with obvious health risks - or is diverted, at a high price, to other countries that gain further economic benefits.

Returning to radioactivity, elements that emit radiation have a highly variable time interval during which their radiation (be it alpha, beta or gamma) is capable of producing measurable effects: the interval ranges from seconds to billions of years. This means that these substances, once used for various purposes, must be disposed of and suitably shielded and isolated in particular environments, rendering them irrelevant from the standpoint of possible biological damage. Some countries are considering a 'geological repository', *i.e.* a deep underground facility that once filled, could be closed and 'forgotten', but only one country has actually built one, Finland. At the moment, nuclear waste is disposed of in surface containers and facilities that are completely safe and constantly controlled.

In the emotional wake of Chernobyl, a referendum in Italy banned the production of nuclear energy in 1987. Italy was the only major country to apply the drastic decision to close all nuclear power plants, while other countries left them open, but didn't build new ones. Italy was preparing to relaunch nuclear power in 2010, but after the tsunami that hit the Japanese Fukushima power plant in March of 2011, another referendum blocked the restart of nuclear energy production. Incidentally, and contrary to what some believe, at Fukushima there was *no* human loss as a result of the accident at the plant, but a large number of deaths (around twenty thousand) caused by the tsunami generated by the earthquake.

In 2025, there are 15 countries in Europe which are planning to restart or initiate nuclear power production. To revive a discussion on nuclear power avoiding a prejudicial approach, it will be necessary to start with an appropriate information campaign. For this, we will have to proceed gradually through education and scientific dissemination, particularly aimed at the younger generations, because they will be the ones who will have to manage future national energy plans. In the end, it is not enough for modern nuclear power to be affordable, safe, green, sustainable and climate-neutral; it must be *perceived* as such. A proper narrative is therefore a priority. And it must be explained that there is the same difference between the Chernobyl plant and the future fourth-generation reactors - about which we will speak shortly - as there is between a clunky car from the 1950s and a technological car of today, equipped with countless active and passive safety systems, which costs less and consumes less and is also much more reliable.

With regard to Fukushima, the controversy that many years later also involved states close to Japan, as well as part of global public opinion, regarding the release of the water that had been used for cooling during the accident, and is now 'technically' even drinkable, was emblematic. The operation, conducted with extreme caution, after careful technical assessments and under the control and endorsement of the International Atomic Energy Agency (IAEA), nevertheless generated strong opposition - spiced with largely irrational fears - albeit without any scientific argument.

As already mentioned, technicians and experts will have to work together with citizens to provide correct information. We will also have to consider the enormous progress in nuclear device technology in recent decades, and then the environmental, economic and social aspects of the energy issue, ensuring that we can deliberate for the overall good of society, taking into account the greater complexity in which we live today and future needs. Energy is precisely one of those issues that directly involve the national interest, such as the welfare state and health care.

Lessons from history

In any case, it should be noted that the principal objections to the use of
the energy from atomic nuclei are not and have not all been justifiable or
made in good faith. Considering only openly disclosed actions, in 1970
Robert Anderson, a leader of the oil industry and head of the Atlantic
Richfield Co., contributed two hundred thousand dollars to fund Friends
of the Earth, an organisation strongly opposed to nuclear energy, citing
problems of both safety and cost.[4] There are many more examples, and
it is understandable that big oil and the fossil fuel industry have over the
decades exploited all possible methods to create an aura of fear (or at least
dissent) towards alternative energy sources such as nuclear or renewables.
It is only natural that the widespread use of such sources would lead to a
substantial reduction in the cost of oil, gas and coal. Today, especially in
the United States, oil is also extracted from shale rock and underwater deposits, disproving what was feared in the 1970s, when it was believed that
oil resources would run out within a few decades. But if the cost of a barrel
fell too far, such (considerably expensive) exploration would no longer be
worthwhile. In any case, about 20 per cent of electricity production in the
US comes from nuclear power, which accounts for more than 60 per cent
of the clean energy produced there. It seems unrealistic to implement, in
America or elsewhere, a serious decarbonisation policy without being able
to count on the contribution of nuclear power. Wind and solar will not be
able to compete with nuclear for this compulsory mission - at least in the
short and medium term.

Then there is the question of research and technological development
for a new generation of nuclear power plants. The United States is at the
forefront with a considerable number of projects, both private and involving the federal government. The goal of 'zero emissions' of CO_2 could be
achieved through a cocktail of green sources, including the nuclear power
of the future, that as we shall see, will be represented by smaller, safer,
cheaper, faster to build and less technologically complex reactors.

As far as research in the field is concerned, it must be said that Italy
too, although outside the club of nuclear nations today, is very active
with its own researchers, at home and abroad, and with its specialised

---

[4] The topic is discussed in a book by F. William Engdahl entitled *Century of War:
Anglo-American Oil Politics and the New World Order* (1992).

companies. This is a subject that has relatively distant roots in the history of our country, beyond the pioneering work of Enrico Fermi and his collaborators during the Manhattan Project. In 1952, Felice Ippolito was appointed secretary of the National Committee for Nuclear Research, a body created at that time, which in 1960 was to become the National Committee for Nuclear Energy (CNEN). Within a few years, Ippolito, whose expertise in geology - the search for uranium deposits - and nascent nuclear engineering was recognised internationally, embarked on an intensive programme of public investment in civil nuclear power. In 1959, the first research reactor was built in Ispra, on the shores of Lake Maggiore in Northern Italy. The investment and support from the Italian public was considerable. Ippolito helped to build the Latina and Garigliano nuclear power plants and the Enrico Fermi power plant in Trino. By 1966, national production of around 4 billion kilowatt hours was reached,[5] making Italy the third largest producer of nuclear electricity in the world. But in 1964, Ippolito was swept up in a judicial enquiry for alleged administrative irregularities at CNEN and this caused quite a stir, both in Italy and abroad. Whether this was linked to undue interference by stakeholders opposed to the development of a skilled Italian nuclear industry is now a matter for historians.

In the wake of Ippolito's programme, our nuclear engineers became among the most highly qualified internationally, and even when the national programme was discontinued following the 1987 referendum, many of them continued to make a name for themselves working in various countries around the world. Today, decades later, the Italian school of nuclear engineers is still one of absolute excellence and there are many teachers and students involved in various specialised courses in Turin, Milan, Bologna, Rome and Pisa, to name but a few of the most prestigious locations. Many of the young Italian engineers are actively and successfully involved in research and development projects including regarding fusion energy, and in some countries, the construction of new power plants. Not

----

[5] *Power* in physics is defined as the amount of energy produced or consumed in a unit of time. One watt therefore corresponds to one joule of energy produced or consumed in one second. To give an idea, a one-kilo object travelling at a speed of one metre per second has an energy of 0.5 joules. Consequently, we can measure energy as: joule = watts × second, or also - more in keeping with our talk about energy - in kilowatt-hours (1,000 watts × hour). Obviously, 1 megawatt hour is equivalent to 1,000 kilowatt hours.

to mention the high-value activities of researchers at ENEA (National Agency for New Technologies, Energy and Sustainable Economic Development) and other companies, such as ENEL, ENI, Sogin, *newcleo* and Ansaldo Nucleare, engaged in activities directly or indirectly related to nuclear power.

This is how it works

Regarding the 'fuel' of reactors,[6] the most common is uranium, a very heavy element that is about a hundred times more abundant in nature than silver. Its atom is composed of 92 protons, joined together by nuclear forces in the dense, compact nucleus, and 92 electrons distributed in a 'probability cloud' around the former. The nucleus of each uranium atom also contains a large number of neutrons: depending on their number, we have the different isotopes of the element uranium.[7] More than 99 per cent of the uranium on Earth, trapped in its crust, consists of the isotope uranium-238 (the number 238 comes from the sum of 92 protons plus a whopping 146 neutrons). This isotope is radioactive, as it emits alpha particles (which as we have seen, have very low penetration), but it is not subject to the fission process, which we will discuss in detail later. The situation is different, considerably, for another isotope, uranium-235, whose nucleus has three fewer neutrons. This may seem like a negligible difference but, due to the bizarre laws of quantum mechanics, its nucleus is more unstable and therefore susceptible to collision with projectile neutrons that cause it to dissociate (fission) into fragments, with the incidental production of other neutrons. Each fission reaction produces two or three additional neutrons, with an average of about 2.5 neutrons per fission. These, in turn, are able to fission other nuclei, and so on, generating a *chain reaction*, with the exponential creation of a large amount of energy. The cause of this energy production is the so-called 'mass defect', the physical reason for which we will discuss in the next chapter.

---

[6] In reality, there is nothing in a nuclear reactor that burns ...

[7] An *isotope* is defined as a variant of a given chemical element that has the same number of electrons and protons, but a different number of neutrons. For example, the gas element helium is called helium-4 because it has two atomic electrons and, in its nucleus, two protons and two neutrons: hence four nuclear particles. Its isotope helium-3 has, as usual, two electrons and two protons, but only one neutron.

Unfortunately, however, the relative abundance of uranium-235 is less than one per cent compared to other isotopes. One is therefore obliged to select it and refine it through complex technological processes: we then speak of uranium *enrichment*. But that is not all. In order to be able to sustain a chain reaction, a possible block of fissile uranium-235 must possess so-called *critical mass*, below which the neutrons generated in fission do not have enough nuclei with which to collide, initiate the chain reaction and generate more neutrons. The critical mass depends on the particular isotopes used, their degree of purity and also the geometry of their positioning. Assuming a sphere of pure uranium-235, this mass is about 45 kilograms.

The first 'uncontrolled' chain reaction took place during the Manhattan Project. The detonation of the Trinity atomic bomb at the Alamogordo range on 15 July 1945 was tangible and tragic proof of the power of the energy contained deep inside the atomic nucleus.

For the sake of completeness, let us note that there is another widely used fissile element, plutonium-239, which is obtained by striking uranium-238 with neutrons, as in target practice, and which can be used both for military purposes and to operate a reactor for civil purposes. Its critical mass is appreciably less than that of fissile uranium-235, about 10 kilograms. In the end, we speak of *subcritical* conditions when, for a mass of fissile material less than the critical mass, the reaction shuts down because not enough neutrons are produced; *critical* conditions, on the other hand, are present when the reaction is self-sustaining and stable, *i.e.* each fission generates practically only one neutron to sustain it; finally, *supercritical* conditions develop if the energy released grows exponentially due to the large number of neutrons created.

The first nuclear reactor, *i.e.* an infrastructure capable of generating energy in a *controlled* manner, was the one built by Enrico Fermi in Chicago, the *Pile-1*. On 2 December 1942, well before the Alamogordo test, Fermi demonstrated that a chain reaction could be managed, producing energy, but without reaching the condition of autonomous and destructive exponential development. It was the beginning of the potential peaceful use of the atom. Other reactor applications quickly followed, as was to be expected in the military field: in 1954, the American submarine *Nautilus* was the first to be equipped with a small nuclear reactor for its propulsion. In the same year, the Russians built the first power station capable of producing electricity in Obninsk, followed by the British one in Sellafield, the first to generate electricity for commercial use. At the time, these were small reactors capable of developing tens or at most a few hundred megawatts of electricity. In this regard, we must distinguish between the thermal power of the reactor, expressed in 'thermal' Megawatts (MWt), and the (smaller) electrical power produced (MWe).

But what is the operating principle of a nuclear reactor? First, let us make it clear that, as a matter of principle, a reactor *can never produce an atomic explosion*, even if bombed or destroyed by a deliberate attack. The few incidents we have discussed have led to conventional explosions, the result of which was to release radioactive fragments into the surrounding environment. The Chernobyl explosion was caused by a build-up of steam and gas, while in Fukushima, hydrogen reacted with oxygen in a chemical explosion.

The first reason for the impossibility of a nuclear reactor explosion is due to the concentration of uranium-235 fuel. Atomic bombs use uranium enriched to at least 90 per cent or even plutonium-239, which is also of high purity. In contrast, in nuclear reactors, uranium is generally enriched to less than 5 per cent, or up to 20 per cent for some future reactors using HALEU (High-Assay Low-Enriched Uranium). These concentrations are insufficient to trigger an explosive chain reaction, but adequate for peaceful use. Moreover, to achieve a nuclear deflagration, the (enriched) fuel must be brought into a supercritical condition, when the chain reaction proceeds autonomously and very rapidly in an uncontrolled manner, with the number of fissions (and neutrons) increasing exponentially in fractions of a microsecond. In nuclear reactors, as we shall see, in addition to the adoption of (low-enriched) uranium, the very design of the core prevents this situation from being reached, also thanks to the use of so-called control rods.

Then there is the matter of the rapid dissipation of heat and radiation. In atomic bombs, fission generates heat in a very short time, resulting in an explosion. In reactors, on the other hand, heat (usable energy) is continuously removed by the cooling system surrounding the 'core', preventing uncontrolled energy build-up. Finally, there are physical reasons that add further safety margins. As the temperature increases while the chain reaction progresses, the speed of the neutrons increases, making them less efficient at developing the reaction further. The general rule applies, therefore, that if a reactor is in a critical condition at room temperature (reactor off), this condition becomes subcritical spontaneously as the temperature increases - and thus as the fission reaction proceeds. Moreover, as the temperature rises, there is thermal expansion of the fissile material. This causes the uranium atoms to 'pull away' from each other, introducing an additional 'inefficiency' factor. In the end, the net result of the operation of a nuclear power plant is the production of heat - part of which generates electricity through the operation of a turbine - the characteristic cloud of water vapour due to its cooling, and a certain amount of waste from the fission reactions taking place in the fissile element rods.

We have just said that one of the crucial aspects of a nuclear reactor is to allow the chain reaction to be managed, stabilising it and preventing it from developing too rapidly, producing an excessive amount of energy in the form of heat; this would potentially melt elements of the device and possibly the core itself containing the fissile material. For this purpose, *control rods* are used, consisting of suitable materials that have the property of absorbing neutrons, thus depressing the development of an uncontrolled reaction. Boron, cadmium, silver and indium are some of the elements used to construct control rods, which can be inserted into (or extracted from) the matrix that makes up the nuclear fuel. This procedure is remarkably safe and automated, as demonstrated by the minimal number of accidents that have occurred in history, normalised to the large number of reactors and the many years during which they have operated.

The other requirement is to 'slow down' the neutrons generated in fission, to make them 'active' in sustaining the chain reaction. In fact, we will see that slow neutrons are very efficient in triggering and developing the chain fission process. We are talking about *thermal neutrons*, so called because their kinetic energy corresponds to that of air molecules at a temperature of about 20°C, at a speed of about one kilometre per second (slow as a manner of speaking...). But the products of fission extend to secondary (or 'fast') neutrons with energies corresponding to speeds as much as a thousand times greater. In this case, special materials such as ordinary water, graphite or heavy water - which unlike its more common sister has an excess neutron in its molecule - are used to slow them down. These substances effectively succeed in reducing the energy of fission neutrons without absorbing them, which would prevent the chain reaction, rather than promote it. Incidentally, the use of water, generally at high pressure, also has the side effect of cooling the reactor, just like a car radiator.

The operation of *slowing down* is very reliable and efficient: fission reactions can be interrupted within seconds, if necessary, by bringing the reactor to a subcritical condition in order to shut it down. It can be understood, therefore, how the operation of a nuclear power plant is the balancing act between moderation and control of the fission process. At this point, the process is triggered: the heat generated in the stable operation of the reactor is used to heat another closed circuit of water that is brought to a boil. The steam drives a turbine, which generates electricity that, in turn, is made available to the transmission and distribution networks. Schematically, the structure and operation of a conventional nuclear reactor is illustrated in Figure 4.

It is important to understand the origin of the heat generated in fissile fuel. First, the kinetic energy of fission products is automatically converted into heat when these fragments collide with neighbouring atoms. In addition, high-energy photons, called gamma rays, are also copiously produced

Figure 4 Simplified diagram of a pressurised water nuclear reactor (the most common model used today)

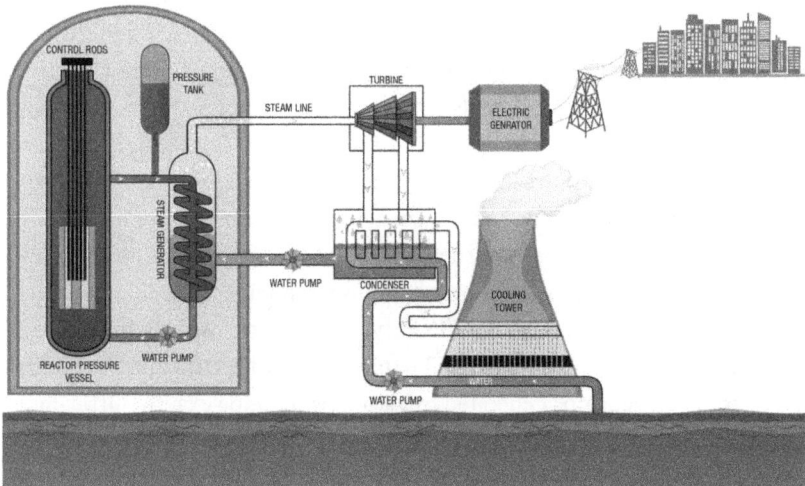

Source: U.S. Department of Energy, Office of Nuclear Energy (https://www.energy.gov/ne/articles/nuclear-101-how-does-nuclear-reactor-work).

in the various nuclear reactions. The mechanical structure of the reactor itself absorbs some of these photons, and again, their energy is converted into heat. Finally, some heat is also generated as a result of the radioactive decay of fission products and materials that have been activated by neutron absorption. This source of decay heat remains active long after the reactor has been shut down. In reality, the diagram shown in Figure 4 is a considerable simplification of the actual way a particular reactor operates. There are many topics of nuclear physics and aspects of device technology (fissile material, its geometrical configuration, moderation and the cooling system) that determine the exact operating parameters of the infrastructure; we will consider the salient ones below.

Particular attention must be paid to the issue of the initial start-up of a reactor. Since this is a machine that in practice works continuously for decades, it appears justified that its 'start-up' is not something as simple as pressing the start button on a car. In fact, it is a complex and highly controlled procedure. Called *first start-up*, it is divided into several steps to ensure that the reactor reaches criticality in a gradual and safe manner. The first step consists of loading the nuclear fuel - usually in the form of uranium-based compound rods - into the reactor's inner structure, the core. The fuel is arranged evenly, while the moderator elements (water or graphite) are usually already present. After loading, the calibration of the neutron detectors, which are essential for subsequent monitoring of the infrastructure, is checked. Then the control rods are fully inserted into the core to make sure that fission reactions cannot start prematurely. The (shutdown) reactor is then in a subcritical condition. Then follows the actual ignition phase: it is necessary to 'light' the fuel with an initial stream of neutrons - a kind of ignition motor - typically emitted by radioactive sources such as americium or californium. The first timid fission reactions are then ignited. The control rods are gradually pulled out and raised to allow more neutrons to propagate the chain reaction. The reactor begins to approach criticality, under very close monitoring of all the machine's physical and technical parameters. Once criticality is reached, the quantity of neutrons generated by fission is set to be exactly sufficient to maintain the chain reaction and make it proceed stably. The reactor is now switched on and is self-sustaining. The generated power gradually increases to the nominal value. At this point, the cooling system is activated to extract the heat produced and transfer it to the steam turbine to finally convert it into electrical energy (Figure 4).

Over the years, developments in nuclear reactor technology have been remarkable, covering all aspects of the technology, from cooling to fuel, from safety to efficiency:

- The *first generation* of reactors included those devices built as advanced prototypes, more like demonstrators, built from the end of the Second World War onwards;
- The *second generation* refers to a class of commercial reactors, cheaper and more reliable than their predecessors, designed to operate stably for several decades. The first were built in the 1960s. Various technologies were used for their cooling: pressurised water, water at atmospheric pressure, liquid sodium and gas. Depending on the models, these reactors have higher or lower levels of automated operation. The power output is thousands of times greater than that of the first reactors; it even exceeds a thousand MWe. A salient feature, due to the long operating life, is the production of radioactive waste (spent fuel), which can be disposed of in underground repositories or be partially reused for the production of new fissile material;
- then there is the *third generation* of reactors, built today, which include design improvements and improvements to the various technologies used: efficiency, fuel, safety systems and computerisation. These improvements are designed to minimise the risk of accidental or premeditated human intervention (Chernobyl) or the extreme cases that characterised the Fukushima accident. These machines are built to operate stably and reliably for up to eighty years before they are decommissioned; the IAEA thinks that it will be possible to achieve up to one hundred years of operation.

The fourth generation will be discussed in Chapter 6. For now, it is important to reiterate that in order to operate a 'conventional' reactor, *slow neutrons* are required - i.e. those with relatively low kinetic energy - which as the chain reaction in uranium or plutonium unfolds, manage to penetrate their atomic nuclei, and like a Trojan horse, almost immediately cause them to dissociate into two or more fragments. In addition to these, a large number of neutrinos are generated (as many as one hundred billion billion per second for a medium-sized device!), the elusive particles that in the universe are second in number only to photons. These neutrinos carry away part of the energy released in reactions without being able to use it, due to their 'reluctance' to interact with ordinary matter. In fact, some of the reactors used for research purposes are aimed precisely at producing and studying neutrinos and have led to very important discoveries.

Fast reactors

In reality - and this is one of the game-changing factors of modern nuclear power plant technology - there is nothing to prevent *fast neutrons* from also being used to support fission reactions. Let us see why.

The probability for a high-energy neutron to fission a uranium-235 nucleus is inherently lower than for a slow neutron (by about six hundred times) but nevertheless, 10 per cent of uranium-238 can be split by a fast neutron. This implies that a normal 'slow' reactor can use a combination of the two isotopes as fuel, with the addition of a moderator. During operation of the device, slow neutrons hitting uranium-238, while not splitting it, contribute to triggering nuclear reactions that eventually generate plutonium-239; this too is fissile under the action of slow neutrons - with much greater probability than uranium-235. But not all plutonium contributes to fission reactions; some of it simply absorbs the slow neutrons and triggers cascades of secondary reactions that lead to the creation of many heavy, radioactive elements that cannot be used as fissile fuel, the waste. Eventually, the 'useful' fuel is consumed, requiring periodic insertion of new enriched uranium and eventual removal of waste.

The situation, which is in fact very complex, becomes appreciably different if we consider a 'fast reactor', still of the third generation, but designed to efficiently exploit precisely the higher-energy neutrons. There are considerable benefits in this case. First, the fast neutrons generated in the fission process are much greater in number than the slow ones. Furthermore, the cooling of the reactor core is achieved by using, for example, salts or liquid metals, such as sodium or lead, since water would act as a moderator by slowing down the neutrons, thus returning us to the case of slow reactors. These elements, unlike water even if it is pressurised (in which case the boiling point increases), have a very wide temperature range within which they are in a liquid state. This makes it possible to effectively cool the reactor up to relatively high temperatures - which could still be reached in the event of a malfunction - thus also increasing the intrinsic safety of the system. It may seem strange to cool a circuit with a liquefied solid metal, but then again, water can also be thought of as liquid ice. Furthermore, since the operating temperatures of a 'fast reactor' are higher than those of a 'slow' one, the efficiency of conversion into usable energy is also higher. This is a thermodynamic property that applies to all types of devices, such as steam or combustion engines, for which the mechanical efficiency depends on the temperature difference between the cold and hot parts of the engine.

The physics of fast reactors is complicated. To simplify, we can say that through a suitable choice of fuel (uranium, plutonium, thorium or even nuclear waste), the reactor can be put into a stable and continuous operating condition. Further, by means of the *breeding* process - the reactor produces more fissile material than it consumes - the device itself creates new fuel during its operation, becoming 'self-fertilising', thus increasing efficiency and optimising the operating cycle by using less new fissile material. Last but not least, the fast neutrons act as 'scavengers' of the waste produced, fissioning - and thus neutralising - the long-lived heavy radioactive elements and making the waste produced more environmentally friendly, with consequently much less stringent management, accumulation and storage requirements.

In one year of operation, a modern 1,000 MWe fast reactor - covering the consumption of a city such as Rome - generates just one tonne of waste, which will remain radioactive for much shorter periods than the waste generated by a reactor using slow neutrons. Within two to three hundred years, these elements will become virtually non-radioactive again, unlike the waste from slow reactors, which can 'live' for hundreds of thousands of years. Moreover, about 10 per cent of this waste is not thrown away at all, as it consists of (non-radioactive) rare earths, which are valuable and needed by the renewable energy industry and beyond. Added to this is the production of high-temperature hydrogen, isotopes for medical use and for so-called nuclear batteries, all very important topics to which we will return in the next chapters. In short, this is a very interesting development indeed.

Fast reactors were already the preferred approach for future nuclear energy technology in the 1970s, initially motivating great optimism for cheap, safe and reliable nuclear power. Consider, for example, the large French Superphénix reactor, which, however, had a troubled life due to initial technical questions (outside the reactor), cost, and above all political problems, until its final shutdown in 1998.[8] The reactor was cooled with liquid sodium. This element has a melting temperature of just 100°C and a high boiling temperature of 900°C, thus presenting an extended operating range and offering high safety standards. Sodium allows heat to be efficiently extracted and transported out of the fuel core and is no more corrosive than water. Its main problem is that, like lithium in mobile phone or car batteries, it ignites upon contact with air and explodes upon contact with water! This feature made Superphénix and its siblings particularly expensive because of the resulting safety systems. Since at the time the cost of a barrel of crude oil fluctuated between $10 and $20 (today it is around $80), it is understandable how the economic justification for such a feat was questioned, not least because of the inability of engineers to come up with reliable technical and economical improvements. But science and technology continued their progress, and from a partial failure, new perspectives soon emerged: using the new generation of fast reactors to achieve a new declination of safe and efficient, as well as economically viable, nuclear power.

After our visit to the American power plant, we leave with the knowledge that it is right and worthwhile to invest in nuclear power for energy production; both in scientific-technological research, and in the creation of new devices that exploit the results of research and meet the requirements for a green, sustainable, safe and cheap source of energy. In the future, we will have to behave like the millions of travellers who take a plane every day for their journeys, as opposed to those who remind us that if a plane crashes you will surely die and prefer a car. But cars cause far more damage and loss of life, although without the sensation of a plane crash. We head straight for the airport, to catch a flight that will take us back to the old continent, to the heart of Europe, which for centuries was itself one of the centres of the world.

In the green Switzerland, in Geneva, there is an international laboratory that everyone knows: CERN. The name, originally an acronym for the European Council for Nuclear Research, was recently changed to the European Laboratory for Particle Physics, due to the fact that subnuclear particle physics is now studied there. The original name dates back to the mid-1950s, when the Centre was founded; but even then, it was very distant from weapons and bombs. Researchers had in fact crea-

---

[8] Here is a video of the dismantling of the French Superphénix machine: https://vimeo.com/439202173

ted the centre with the scientific objective of unlocking the secrets of nature through the study of the atomic nucleus and its constituent particles. This is an example that should make us reflect on how science and technology and their fruits should be exclusively aimed at knowledge or uses of interest to society.

CERN is the ideal place to continue our chat about energy from the nucleus and its many useful and peaceful applications, and to understand a little more about the physical nature of the subatomic microcosm.

3   CERN Geneva, Switzerland

A Bit of Atomic Physics

CERN's canteen is one of those places that has acquired a particular reputation over time, certainly among the physicists who frequent this great laboratory on the outskirts of Geneva or one of the other great centres of elementary particle physics in the world. The popular belief - which, in the end, reflects the reality quite well - is that many of the scientific activities that take place in the Geneva laboratory benefit from the discussions among physicists that take place here, over a coffee or a drink at one of the small tables in the garden, with drawings and sketches of calculations or hypothetical experiments, perhaps sketched on paper napkins. Be that as it may, this special social habitat, where thousands of researchers work to discover the innermost secrets of matter, space and time, began over seventy years ago with the formation of the CERN, thanks to the lucid madness of a small handful of European scientists, coordinated by Pierre Auger and Edoardo Amaldi.

The birth of CERN was, in fact, a clear example of how the community of scientists, especially the community of nuclear physicists - many of whom had played an active role in the creation of the weapons used during the first half of the 20th century - succeeded in bonding around objectives of peace and international cooperation. CERN built a bridge between war and peace, between the use of technology and science for military purposes and that oriented towards knowledge and the welfare of society. The laboratory saw the light of day just nine years after the end of the Second World War. The conflict had left ruins, and not only in the literal sense of the word, having also destroyed any possible faith in a future Europe that could be built on principles of peace, equality and fraternity between peoples. Political Europe had to be rebuilt, but there were too many wounds still open, and relations between the major nations were difficult, to say the least, even simply due to the fact that they had been fighting each other just a few years earlier. Fortunately, however, a tenuous thread of contact, if not collaboration, had remained in place between European scientists, albeit from conflicting countries.

With foresight and determination, they were able to look beyond their differences. The idea was to restart collaboration between European nations through science and to use nuclear physics to achieve this end. With a seemingly unbelievable approach, they decided to use what in the collective imagination was considered the ultimate expression of the power of war, represented by the Hiroshima and Nagasaki disasters. Their proposal was to take the power of modern science out of the purely warlike sphere and bring it back into the realm of human knowledge, using the most advanced physics at the time, that of the atomic nucleus. This, apart from its military application, constituted the frontier of knowledge of nature at its deepest level.

Since then, science has moved forward, and nuclear physics has evolved into the physics of its constituents and sub-constituents: modern particle physics. But even today, the link between nuclear physics, energy and particles is very strong at CERN, with the understanding that possible military applications are simply and categorically banned, that all results obtained by scientists are immediately made public, and that any developments of an applicative nature are made freely available to society. One example demonstrates the point: the invention of the World Wide Web, which took place at CERN in the late 1980s.

Today, as in the days of the founding of CERN, we are facing a new cultural and societal challenge: rethinking the concept of energy for a prosperous and sustainable future. The new energy 5.0 will be an important key to realising this dream, but the strength and enthusiasm of future generations will have to do the rest.

Einstein's petrol

The concept of energy, at its deepest level, is central to everything at CERN, as it underpins every possible scientific-technological consideration. And in speaking of energy, following in the footsteps of Lavoisier, the saying he formulated with reference to every chemical reaction applies: 'No energy is created or destroyed', but all energy is only transformed from one form to another. Scientists summarise this by saying that the energy of a given physical (or even biological) system is subject to a *conservation principle*: there is as much of it at the beginning as there is at the end of all the processes that may occur. Let us think, for example, of a system consisting of a large room in which a car is stationary. We can reasonably assume that the initial energy of the system is that corresponding to the 50 litres of petrol in the car's tank. Let us then imagine that we start the vehicle and drive it around the room until all the petrol is consumed. What will be the energy of our system in the end? It will be equal to the amount of heat present in the environment (heat, as mentioned, is also a form of energy): heat accumulated in the engine, in the air with the combustion fumes, in the walls of the room that are now hotter. Even the noise (sound waves) produced in the operation of the engine must be included. Doing the math in detail, the sum of all these quantities of energy will be just the same as that accumulated in 50 litres of fuel. But what happened, instant by instant, while the car was in motion moving within our system? In that case, the energy of the initial 'fill-up' was exactly equal to that of the remaining petrol, the heat and noise that had already been produced, and the kinetic (or motion) energy of the moving vehicle. If this had hit an obstacle, setting it in motion, we would also have had to consider its kinetic energy. Thus, we understand that the principle of conservation of energy, a cornerstone of science, is not just one of those laws of nature engraved on marble but is also useful for understanding and quantitatively studying everything that happens around us, assuming its absolute and proven validity.

A first conclusion we draw is that it is improper to speak of 'consumption' of energy; rather, one should mean its *utilisation*. What may be consumed are the elements that allow energy to be 'stored', such as the petrol in the previous example, an electric battery or coal in a furnace. In our society, we often create a logical short-circuit, confusing energy with those elements and substances that allow it to become manifest: fuels, an electric battery, oil, gas and so on. This may sound like a woolly question, but it is not.

Leaving a rigorous definition aside for the moment, we can ask: "But what is energy used for?" The first obvious answer would be: "To heat us and our homes, to make vehicles of various kinds move and - why not? - to keep us and all living organisms alive through food, which is, after all, another form of energy storage. It is no coincidence that in quantifying the energy intake of a certain food we speak of calories, and heat - we repeat - is itself a form of energy. In reality, the situation is more complex. Energy also serves to 'build things', including all living things, whether plants or animals. This aspect is unintuitive, but of substantial importance. Build-

ing a house means assembling materials. In some cases, the materials are
available in nature and only need to be cut, shaped or treated appropriately,
such as wood. And it is implicit that energy is needed for all these opera-
tions: to operate the tools, saws or milling cutters, or even for technicians
and workers to perform their manual actions. In other cases, however, the
materials of our house must be created from nothing, if you can call it that,
or better still, be produced by combining indistinct elements, again thanks
to energy: bricks, pipes, steel beams and cement. Incidentally, cement factories are particularly energy-intensive and also producers of large quantities of carbon dioxide, the primary cause of global warming. Cement
production requires energy to both operate the equipment and to carry out
the chemical reactions involved in the creation of composite substances,
such as the cement itself.

It also takes energy to grow a tree, a cow or a new human being; to
make trousers or to bake bread; to run, eat or digest; even to think. In
short, to have built the world we find ourselves in today, it has been
necessary to use an inordinate amount of energy, drawn from the various
sources where it is stored, starting with fossil fuels. To give a general
idea, let us recall that about 30 per cent of the world's energy consumption today is due to industry, 28 per cent to commercial transport and
another 42 per cent to everything else, including our biological and domestic needs. And it is precisely that 30 per cent related to industry that
poses and will pose the most quantitatively relevant questions in relation
to decarbonisation.[1]

Thus, every natural activity - including those involving both living and
non-living matter - that can ultimately be traced back to some form of
action or movement, requires an expenditure of energy. And such energy
can never be created out of nothing - it takes energy to obtain energy! -
but will have to be found at the expense of different forms of energy. Let
us imagine, for example, a rolling bowling ball. It possesses energy due to
its movement, which is transformed into that of the pins once hit; but the
ball's energy comes from the energy transferred by our arm, which in turn
has been transferred from the energy 'stored' in the food ingested before
the game. Needless to say, by correctly adding up all the various forms of
energy and those of their transfer, we always obtain a perfect balance, as in

---

[1] See the page updated in real time https://www.iea.org/world/energy-mix?utm_
source

the example of the car. In this regard, it is worth noting that in the early days of mankind, the main source of energy was precisely that produced by us, by the strength of our muscles, or by harnessing the strength of domestic animals employed in field work or in battle. Then came other discoveries that paved the way for a relentless search for new sources of energy, a search that is far from over today, driven by a continuous demand to support our ever-increasing needs.

At this point, we can try to give a somewhat more rigorous definition. Energy, the fundamental quantity of physics and the engine of the universe at both the infinitesimal and cosmological scales, is defined as the *capacity to perform mechanical work*, producing displacements and motion of bodies, whether large, small or even microscopic, or even *to generate heat*. Energy continually changes its appearance through the infinite transformations that characterise all physical/chemical/biological processes, where in each guise there is generally a movement, an action, and a displacement involved. Physicists have characterised the concept of energy by defining kinetic and potential energy, and then chemical, electrical, thermal and radiant energy.

But we cannot fail to mention that the real complication, if not revolution, came with Albert Einstein's theory of relativity in 1905: $E=mc^2$. This equivalence shows us that energy and mass are 'interchangeable', proportional to each other by means of a very large number: the square of the speed of light c, which has the astronomical value of three hundred thousand kilometres per second, such that it is possible to reach the Moon in one second or the Sun in just over eight minutes. Einstein's equation truly deserves its fame: it expresses in a simple and elegant manner the *equivalence of mass and energy* and sanctions the possibility of transforming the former into the latter (and the latter into the former). Mass thus becomes a kind of energy concentrate, an important element of the energy budget of a material object or particle. Even small values of mass can give rise to enormous amounts of energy. In completely converting a single gram of matter into energy, we obtain an energy equal to that released by the explosion of 21,000 tonnes of TNT! The crucial question then becomes *how to* transform mass into energy.

The particle accelerator that occupies the 27-kilometre-long, circular underground tunnel that we walk through, alongside long dipole magnets and superconducting cryogenic elements, physically identifies the main experimental activity conducted by CERN physicists. The Large Hadron Collider (LHC), the largest and most complex machine ever built by man, the record-setting accelerator, is the jewel in the Centre's crown. In the large particle physics laboratory, subatomic corpuscles injected into the accelerator's vacuum tube are carried up to almost the speed of light, providing them with high kinetic energy thanks to variable electric fields – all for entirely peaceful purposes. The very tiny particles acquire energies that are small on the human scale, but enormous when concentrated in a microscopic entity, such as an atom, an atomic nucleus or an elementary particle. The 'energised' particles are then made to collide. In the collision, part of their energy is transformed into mass - thanks to Einstein's relation - and new particles are 'created from nothing', in the literal sense of the term. This is the exact opposite of what happens when mass is transformed into energy: new, previously non-existent particles appear from the energy of the colliding particles.

By studying the characteristics of such 'events', physicists are able to reconstruct the gigantic puzzle of nature, leading other pieces to fit into a picture that over the years is becoming increasingly clear (and intriguing): the picture of the structure of matter, space-time and the forces that act between particles and mysteriously bind the infinitely small and the immensely large of the cosmos in a picture that now appears coherent and unifying. It is important to reiterate the fact that Einstein's equation, when travelled in one direction, generates energy, while in the other it allows for the creation of matter - truly fascinating!

However, there is another reason to accelerate particles and provide them with great energy. The greater the energy in the collision, the smaller the dimensions that can be explored. In the days of the first accelerators in the 1950s, one could barely 'observe' the atomic nucleus, whereas today, thanks to the LHC, we are able to study the constituents of protons and neutrons themselves (quarks), which show us a structure of matter similar to that of Russian dolls. However, the structure and physics of the atomic nucleus had already become quite clear to physicists by the late 1920s.

Nuclear billiards

Energy of nuclear origin is naturally derived from the physical prerogatives of the microcosm, through the practical application of Einstein's mass-energy equivalence. First, we observe that the energy we require for our various needs can be found at 'zero kilometres': on our own planet. Its source is always the Sun, though, either directly, through electromagnetic radiation, light and heat, or indirectly, through its various manifestations and transformations: fossil fuels, wind or sea waves. Then there is another quantitatively considerable source of energy: nuclear energy, generated by the fission of the nuclei of heavy radioactive elements such as uranium or plutonium. These elements are not a product of the operation of the Sun but come from past cosmic cataclysms such as the bursting of supernovae, stars at the end of their life cycle, or immense collisions between neutron stars. In the former case, in the final phase of their functioning, before the catastrophic burst, stars manage to produce all the heavy elements we find here on Earth, especially uranium. It is truly amazing to think that we humans are literally children of the stars!

The atom is the 'quantum' object par excellence, which cannot be ascribed to a 'classical' vision, *i.e.* one based on the laws of late 19th century physics: mechanics, electrodynamics and thermodynamics. For its understanding, physicists in the early 20th century were reluctantly forced to develop quantum mechanics, a theory that is highly counterintuitive, probabilistic and capable of violating the 'sacrosanct' principle of causality. Nevertheless, we can try to get an idea of atomic structure and dimensions by making 'classical' comparisons. If the circumference of the hydrogen atom, defined by the average orbit of its single electron, were equal to that of the outer perimeter of a football stadium, then the electron would be a speck of dust and the atomic nucleus a peppercorn placed on the centre field disk. Put simply, matter, although it often appears very rigid to us, is essentially 'empty' on a microscopic scale. Numerically, the diameter of an atom averages about ten billionths of a centimetre (10^{-8} cm) and that of a nucleus one thousandth of a billionth of a centimetre (10^{-12} cm). The size of the electron is virtually zero, although its mass, which is in any case very small, is not. In contrast, the proton and neutron are particles with a well-defined size of 10^{-13} cm. Their mass is about two thousand times greater than that of the electron. It is therefore understood that the approximation of considering the mass of the atom as concentrated in its nucleus is entirely well-founded. As an aside, this fact justifies the name *nuclear energy*, rather than atomic *energy*, since all reactions take place within the nucleus.

One of the many problems that beset the early atomic and nuclear physicists was that they lacked a theory that could explain the structure and stability of the nucleus, and that there was the possibility that certain atoms - nuclei, we would say today - could emit radiation, either spontaneously or stimulated by collisions with other particles. We have seen that such radiation can be of three types: *alpha* (particles consisting of two protons and two neutrons stuck together, *e.g.* a helium nucleus), *beta* (consisting of electrons) and *gamma* (consisting of photons also of relatively high energy). The question that immediately arose for the physicists of the last century was what the origin and mechanism of these emissions were. In the case of beta radiation, for example, it certainly could not be the electrons that make up the cloud around the nucleus, their energy being thousands of times lower than that measured. It must therefore have been radiation originating in the nucleus, where the energies involved reach much higher values. Today we know that a 'free' neutron, after an average time of about 900 seconds, spontaneously decays (transforms) into a proton, an electron and a neutrino. In contrast, neutrons bound together with protons in the atomic nucleus - and therefore no longer free - generally cannot decay due to complex physics issues relating to the principle of energy conservation, unless they are in 'unstable nuclei' - known as *radioactive* nuclei. In this case, the energy balance of the reaction is favourable, and beta electrons can therefore be emitted, even with a fair amount of energy. This generally happens in neutron-rich nuclei - heavy elements, such as uranium or plutonium, in particular for some of their isotopes. Eventually, it became clear that the three types of radiation (alpha, beta and gamma) were all due to reactions involving the atomic nucleus alone.

Speaking of atoms, nuclei and radiation may like seem a complex subject - and perhaps it is - but it is important in order to understand the origin of the energy hidden in the nucleus of the atom, where the nuclear reaction most closely linked to energy considerations, in particular the possibility of obtaining energy from it, is that of fission. Particularly heavy and unstable nuclei of atoms, either spontaneously or through collisions with other particles, can break up and fragment into lighter nuclei, thus assimilating different elements from the initial one. In such a reaction, which is exothermic in that it generates energy, in addition to the fragments gaining considerable kinetic energy, gamma rays and individual particles, particularly neutrons, can be created. When slow neutrons - which, as we have said, have a speed of a few kilometres per second - manage to enter the nucleus of particular so-called *fissile* elements, they disrupt their energy balance, leading to dissociation. The mechanism is similar to that whereby a drop of water (the nucleus in our case) subjected to pressure stretches until it splits at the point where it becomes thinner, thus creating two new, smaller drops of water.

Once produced, the two nuclei generated by the fission, being positively charged, rapidly move apart due to the strong electromagnetic repulsion. The process is not comparable to radioactive decay, as it involves the complete dissociation of the nucleus. A key aspect is that the sum of the masses of all the fruits of the reaction, the two or more nuclear fragments plus the various neutrons – that this time are relatively energetic - is significantly less than that of the starting nucleus. The equation $E = mc^2$ does the rest: the even small difference in mass corresponds to a very large amount of energy released in a very short time. And, as if this were not enough, the neutrons generated can in turn induce other fissions in the material, in what is known as a *nuclear chain reaction*. The control of such a reaction led, as we have seen, to the invention of nuclear reactors by Enrico Fermi, reactors capable of using the heat generated in the process to transform water into high-temperature steam, which in turn can produce electricity thanks to a special turbine. However, under certain conditions that are fortunately not very probable, leaving the chain reaction free to unleash itself in an uncontrolled manner can cause the sum of the energies created for each nuclear fission to cause the sudden production of explosive energy: thus, we have the nuclear weapon.

For reference, we note that the amount of energy potentially contained in a certain mass of a nuclear 'fuel' element is millions of times greater than that associated with, say, an equal amount of petrol, effectively making the energy of the atomic nucleus extremely cheap. This is further proof that mass, by virtue of Einstein's relativity, is a true condensate of energy and that the energy stored in the nucleus is correspondingly high. Moreover, since fission is facilitated by the relatively low energy of the incident neutrons, the secondary neutrons produced as a result of fission, possessing a significantly higher energy, must be 'moderated' (slowed down) in order to sustain the chain reaction. This is achieved by making them lose speed through collisions with protons, just like balls on a billiard table. For this purpose, hydrogen-rich materials are used, whose nuclei are in fact mere protons. Water, which contains hydrogen, is a typical moderator used in nuclear power plants, also performing the ancillary task of cooling the fissile fuel. Conversely, in order to prevent the reaction from developing in an uncontrolled manner together with the elements of uranium, plutonium or thorium, the aforementioned control rods are placed in the reactor core, consisting of special substances that effectively absorb part of the neutrons.

Thus, one realises the physical and technological complexity behind the operation of a nuclear power plant - at least those in operation today. However, we repeat, nuclear energy is *neutral* in relation to the current climate crisis, since in the operation of a reactor there is no production of greenhouse gases: in a nuclear reactor, the heat generated by the many reactions that take place in the atoms of the fuel is used, but nothing is burnt. Therefore, there is no particulate matter, and no CO_2 to contribute to the greenhouse effect, but the simple release of the immense energy stored billions of years ago in the depths of matter and now available to mankind. This property will increasingly become a decisive element in strategic energy decisions of the future.

Attaching nuclei

The other mechanism, which is also clean and does not generate greenhouse gases, and which can produce immense amounts of energy, is *fusion*, basically the reverse of fission. In this case, nuclei of light atoms fuse together to form nuclei of greater mass. If nuclei of elements lighter than iron fuse together - we will see later why this is so - energy is released in even greater quantities than in the case of fission, again because of the mass defect. Nuclear fusion is the basis for the functioning of stars, including our Sun, and to date - unfortunately - has only been successfully replicated by mankind in thermonuclear devices, called hydrogen bombs for this reason. Controlled fusion for energy production for civil purposes is still far off, despite the efforts of researchers.

But what is the physical process by which nuclei of light elements can fuse to form new, heavier nuclei? The explanation is somewhat complex, but certainly intriguing (Figure 5). In the emblematic case of stars, it is a series of very unlikely and in some ways fortunate reactions that ensure the long and stable functioning of stars. At the centre of stars, temperatures are extremely high, as high as 15 million degrees Celsius and more. Under these conditions, the hydrogen gas nuclei (single protons) are excited at an energy corresponding to a speed of more than 2.5 million kilometres per hour! Having a positive electrical charge, the many protons in strong agitation tend to repel each other violently. But something special hap-

Figure 5   Schematic diagram of the main nuclear fusion reactions in the Sun: first, the fusion of two hydrogen nuclei generates a deuterium nucleus; this, in turn, may fuse with another hydrogen nucleus to form the helium-3 isotope, and so on.

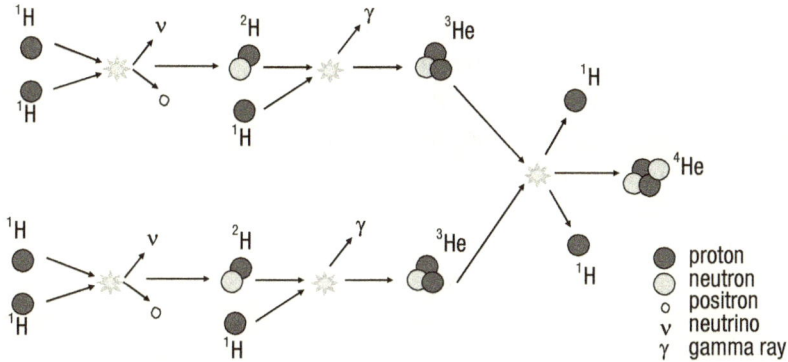

pens if, by chance, two of them come particularly close together. Although in this case the electromagnetic barrier increases enormously, tending to exert a very intense repulsive force (due to the positive electric charge of both), a process typical of quantum mechanics known as the *tunnel effect* may come into play, whereby the two protons manage to attach to each other. However, such a system is very unstable and most of the time the two protons dissociate again. In a tiny fraction of cases, however, one of the two particles, prior to dissociation, may 'have time' to transform into a neutron plus a positive electron plus a neutrino, thanks to a very unlikely 'reverse beta decay'.

At this point, however, the proton-neutron system is stable. A deuterium nucleus has been created, a kind of (heavy) hydrogen, which compared to the ordinary hydrogen nucleus has an extra neutron. The neutrino quickly escapes towards the outside of the star; the positive electron is immediately 'annihilated' with one of the many negative electrons from the surrounding hydrogen atoms. In the end, adding up all the energies produced, the deuterium production reaction brings a a surplus of energy for each nuclear fusion reaction. Without going into the complex details, the deuterium nucleus can in turn fuse with another free proton and form a new stable nucleus, the helium-3 isotope, consisting of two protons and a neutron, still emitting energy in the form of a photon. By now the game is up. Larger and larger nuclei are built according to a series of cascading reactions, which are known as the *proton–proton chain*.

There are other, less significant chains, but they all contribute to the extremely stable condition of the star. As mentioned, the sun has been shining uninterruptedly for five billion years and still has five more to go. And it is certainly to the credit of scientists that they have understood the complicated physics behind the sun's majestic light and the romantic twinkling of other stars!

In the nuclear fusion that occurs deep inside stars, therefore, immense amounts of energy are emitted in the form of light, heat and neutrinos, in a slow and steady process. Hydrogen, the starting element, is very common in the universe. It makes up roughly 75 per cent of all the components in the cosmos, while helium makes up almost all of the remaining 25 per cent. Both elements were produced shortly after the Big Bang by virtue of the extremely high temperatures (or, equivalently, energy densities) of the newly-born universe. The fusion of hydrogen nuclei into helium nuclei that occurs in the myriads of stars in the cosmos continually adds more helium. The creation of gradually heavier nuclei proceeds for billions of years in the fiery stars. Eventually, all the elements that we find on Earth and that also make up our bodies are generated: principally, oxygen, nitrogen and carbon.

As mentioned, the exothermic chain of element formation stops at iron; later atoms in the periodic table are not produced because much more energy would need to be supplied for them from outside. They are generated in another way, namely by the bursting of supernovae, the final state of functioning of certain stars which, having run out of hydrogen fuel, may experience a very turbulent phase at the end of their lives, concluding with a huge explosion of immeasurable energy. These explosions, which are very common in the cosmos as a whole, fertilise galactic space with heavy elements, useful to possible life forms around the cosmos and with great energy releases, in many cases 'petrol' for the fantastic phenomena that occur in the deep universe. From the point of view of the energy associated with such cosmic cataclysms, we are faced with impressive numbers: we are typically talking about an energy equivalent to that emitted by the sun in its entire life of ten billion years but generated in just a few seconds!

In any case, a fully functioning star is the balance point between the outward emission of energy, due to the powerful thermonuclear reactions taking place in its central core, and the gravitational force that tends to collapse the mass of incandescent gas, which constitutes the matter of which the star is composed. The energies involved in the functioning of stars, understood as gigantic thermonuclear furnaces, are impressive. We have seen that in the Sun six hundred million tonnes of hydrogen are transformed into helium every second. The mass difference of four million tonnes per second is converted according to Einstein's equation into a small part of the photons that bring heat and light to Earth. The total power emitted by the Sun is immense for our energy scales: 4×10^{27} watts, about 250 billion times the energy consumption of all mankind. And, despite the distance of 150 million kilometres, the Sun generates a power of 1,400 watts per square metre on Earth. But that is not all. About three per cent of the energy produced by the Sun goes into a gigantic number of neutrinos; the Sun produces so many that every square centimetre of the Earth's surface is crossed by more than sixty billion solar neutrinos per second. It is really quite fortunate for us living beings that their probability of interaction with matter, including biological matter of course, is completely negligible! It is also interesting to note that neutrinos are a 'by-product' of the operation of both nuclear reactors and all the stars in the firmament.

Finally, let us return to the possibility of artificially creating nuclear fusion and consequently producing energy. As mentioned, the first human realisation of the process took place in the early 1950s with the invention of the thermonuclear bomb (called the H-bomb). We have seen that in order to trigger the fusion reactions, very high temperatures are required in the centre of the stars; we are talking about well over ten million degrees, which is completely impossible to achieve on Earth with any kind of thermal combustion process, unless a 'normal' nuclear fission bomb is used to generate the temperature necessary to trigger the fusion reactions in a disruptive and uncontrolled manner. This is precisely what happens in an H-bomb: in the device, the trigger is nothing more than a conventional atomic bomb to reach the very high temperatures needed for fusion. It sounds absurd, but unfortunately it works.

Of a different tenor, fortunately, are the attempts for the peaceful use of the process, such as the idea of recreating on Earth the immense power of the Sun to generate large amounts of clean and renewable energy; a real dream for generations of physicists who have undertaken ambitious and complex projects in recent decades. By means of a safe and reliable mechanism, nuclei of light elements such as deuterium, present in very small doses in normal water, and tritium, artificially produced in nuclear reactors, can fusion at very high temperatures, creating nuclei of heavier elements and thus generating large amounts of thermal energy that is then converted into electricity, but without the generation of radioactive spent fuel. The problems in building such a reactor[2] are mainly techno-logical: how to achieve the required temperatures and how to contain the plasma (the very high temperature gas) that must permanently produce thermal energy. Needless to say, no container made of metal, or any oth-er material, can withstand a temperature of millions of degrees. Intense magnetic fields are then used to 'levitate' the glowing gas, which in turn is 'heated' by laser beams or high-power electromagnetic waves. The cur-rent problem, which is far from trivial, is to eventually obtain more ener-gy than is needed to trigger and sustain the fusion reaction, resulting in a 'net energy gain'.

Despite all these problems, scientists have obtained encouraging results in recent years that bode well for future success. The problem is that, even assuming that fusion can be achieved experimentally, it will be necessary to find out whether it will be economically viable and, in any case, it will take a long time to spread its industrial use, which is by nature very cen-tralised, as it requires complex infrastructures to ignite the reaction and contain the gas at very high temperatures. Given the complexity of such systems and the high cost of the sophisticated components required, it re-mains to be seen how commercially viable it will be to use fusion. If these problems are solved in the coming decades, the effort will undoubtedly pay off: a single litre of water used to generate energy from nuclear fusion - thanks to the deuterium it contains - is equivalent to as much as three hundred litres of oil.

However, it is reasonable to assume that for the next thirty to forty years and perhaps more, the core energy for all practical, civil and industrial pur-poses will remain next-generation fission energy, capable of constituting adequate energy portfolios. As we shall see, the benefits will also be eco-

---

[2] If you want to get an idea of what it looks like, go to 'The Machine' section on the website of ITER, the international research centre based in France that is developing the tokamak project (https://www.iter.org/machine).

nomic, since a sustainable and effective cycle can be proposed that includes all aspects regarding the use of this energy, from medicine to technology and innovation, and from social to political implications as well.

In any case, the issue of tritium supply deserves some attention. As mentioned, this element is very rare in nature, and current supplies would not allow widespread use of fusion for commercial purposes. It would still be essential to use dedicated nuclear fission reactors to produce the needed quantities of tritium, or, complicating the project, to use future fusion reactors themselves to generate the tritium they need. Another possibility would be to use other light elements for fusion reactions. For example, there are ongoing projects investigating the use of hydrogen and boron, or deuterium and helium-3, the rare isotope of helium. But such reactions require much higher temperatures to be reached than for deuterium-tritium (even hundreds of millions of degrees), greatly amplifying the technological problems to be addressed and solved.

Finally, there is also a technical issue that will have to be resolved in order to make future nuclear fusion power plants viable in practice. The extremely high plasma temperatures cause a huge amount of energy to be released in the form of heat and neutrons. The fusion machines being planned are designed to confine the deuterium fuel by means of magnetic fields, but they can do nothing against the neutrons generated in the fusion reactions, as they are electrically neutral and therefore not subject to magnetic confinement. These neutrons, however, unlike those produced in fission reactors, have a very high energy. Apart from the safety issues that would impose considerable shielding systems - feasible, in any event - these neutrons can damage or almost fill the reactor's inner walls with microscopic holes. In the long run, such holes would not only undermine the integrity of the reactor's inner wall, but also create microscopic channels through which deuterium and tritium could permeate. Since tritium is rare and expensive, this is to be avoided; a further problem that needs to be addressed and resolved before the commercial exploitation of fusion power plants. This situation, once again, leads us to consider the not-so-distant future of next-generation fission energy.

In life, coincidences happen and matter, even more so when it comes to encounters between people. In this case, it was an event that many years later would lead us to share these reflections of ours with you. Coincidence would have it that, in two CERN surface laboratories not far from the LHC tunnel where we are now, in

the early 1990s we were both working on projects straddling nuclear and particle physics. Antonio was developing a new type of detector for measuring particle energy: the 'spaghetti calorimeter', with thin scintillating fibres embedded in a
lead matrix. The operating principle of the detector was based on various nuclear
reactions involving neutrons, reactions that achieved the device's excellent performance in terms of energy resolution. Stefano, on the other hand, was involved in
a study that saw particle physics applied to the production of clean, green nuclear
energy. In that case, the original idea of Carlo Rubbia, Nobel Prize winner for physics and at the time director of the Geneva laboratory, was to harness the energy of
protons accelerated by a machine at CERN, in a reactor containing heavy elements such as thorium, plutonium or uranium, to activate nuclear reactions that would
eventually allow more energy to be obtained than was needed to run the accelerator,
hence the name 'energy amplifier'. This research also yielded very interesting results, beyond the practical possibility of using particle accelerators in combination with
nuclear reactors. The success of the two studies supports the idea that different
fields of scientific research can be combined in a virtuous manner to realise application projects of general interest to society, according to the 'magic' paradigm of
transdisciplinarity.

But now we leave CERN and board a tram that will take us to the Cornavin Station, where we will hop on a train to France. This train, passing an underwater tunnel about twice as long as the LHC, will take us into the heart of a major European
metropolis.

4   City of London, United Kingdom
For Sustainable Decarbonisation

At a stone's throw from St. Paul's Cathedral, in the bustling centre of a London no longer as foggy as it was a few decades ago, but still somewhat polluted by industrial emissions, we find the London Stock Exchange. This is London's financial market, which although surpassed by New York's Wall Street after World War II, has played a key role in the world economy for centuries., although surpassed. The Intercontinental Exchange has its office just a few hundred metres away; it is the London branch of an Atlanta-based company that manages the set of financial products backed by the black gold of the North Sea, the famous barrel of Brent crude oil. The large undersea deposit of Brent is shared by the UK with Belgium, Denmark, France, Germany, Norway and the Netherlands. These countries, through their public and private companies, operate around two hundred oil platforms similar to the one we visited in the Gulf of Mexico.

North Sea oil, which began to be extracted not so long ago, in 1966, is now the international standard due to its high quality. The oil crisis of the early 1970s favoured its extraction, not only because of its quality, but also because of the political stability of the region, shared by allied European countries with relatively common goals. But we have already discussed oil. What we want to emphasise now is that global finance investors negotiate commodity contracts on Brent crude as a hedge or on a speculative basis, in connection with the many companies that produce and market crude oil, and the refineries or industries that process it. These procedures, which are more or less the same in the City, in Wall Street or in the other major financial centres of the world, also apply to the many other companies in the energy sector, and quite recently, to those active in the renewable energy sector and the 'green economy'. Moreover, there is a growing interest around the development of new technologies in the field of energy. And if finance has scented a bargain, it means that something is really moving in the world of industry, and more broadly as well.

Money and wallets

In April 2024, Olkiluoto 3, the first new nuclear reactor to be switched on in Europe for more than 15 years, went into operation in Finland. Within just a few days, the price of electricity in the country dropped by 75 per cent, from 246 euros per Megawatt-hour in December 2023 to 61 euros in April 2024. Finland had faced a considerable energy crisis after banning energy imports from neighbouring Russia as part of the reaction to the invasion of Ukraine. The energy from Olkiluoto 3 was not only cheap, but also green, in accordance with the well-known sensitivity of Northern European states towards environmental issues. On the other hand, Finland's choice is understandable considering the country's specificities: it is difficult to think of solar energy, for example, due to the low insolation and long dark months during the Arctic winter. Furthermore, renewable energies such as hydro, solar or wind power require storage and distribution systems to take into account their inherently 'intermittent' nature. If solar panels operate only during the day, their production capacity is reduced to less than 25% of the nominal installation value, also imposing complex (and expensive) storage systems during the day and distribution systems for the night. The reduction of efficiency in the production of electricity from the various sources is well quantified by the so-called capacity factor, a quantity that indicates the percentage of energy that is generated in a given time interval compared to the maximum amount that can be produced (Figure 6). It is understandable that nuclear has the highest value and solar the lowest: a reactor produces energy continuously, with minimal technical interruptions, while the operation of solar panels is linked to insolation, obviously during daylight hours only.

In this regard, it is emblematic of recent news that in California, where private homes enjoy considerable insolation and a large number of photovoltaic systems have been installed, some of the electricity produced during 'peak hours' is literally lost due to grid overload. It is estimated that about 3 Megawatt-hour are lost per year, also due to the high cost of possible storage batteries.

Figure 6   Capacity factor of nuclear, gas, coal, hydro, wind and solar (USA, 2019)

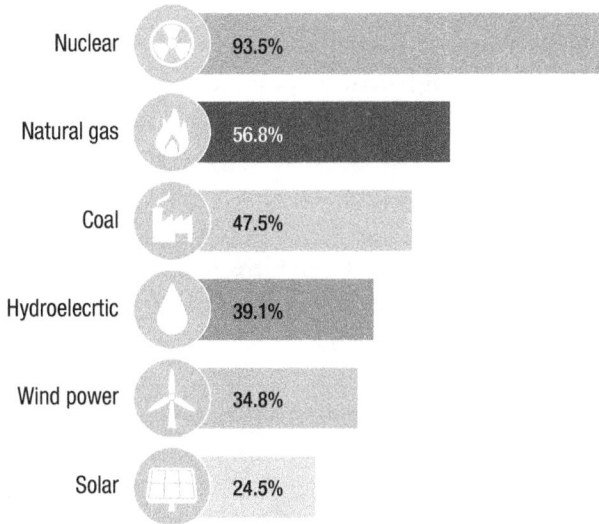

Nuclear	93.5%
Natural gas	56.8%
Coal	47.5%
Hydroelecrtic	39.1%
Wind power	34.8%
Solar	24.5%

Source: U.S. Department of Energy, Office of Nuclear Energy (https://www.energy.gov/ne/arti-cles/infographic-capacity-factor-energy-source-2019).

Moreover, both solar and wind power, like all other energy sources, whether renewable or not, green or CO_2 producing, offer advantages but also disadvantages, in addition to their intermittent nature. Wind turbines disfigure the landscape, generate noise and threaten many species of birds. Solar photovoltaics also impact the landscape and require a great deal of land and material consumption, resulting in the use of many mineral re-sources and the need for relatively frequent disposal of the panels, which is complex and costly. The message we have already given many times is that in the field of future energy there is no magic wand; all energy sourc-es offer advantages and disadvantages, which in turn vary from country to country. The only viable approach is therefore to build *balanced energy portfolios that are protected* from possible problems associated with one or another source of supply.

The world's most economically and technologically advanced states, in particular, must today address the issue of energy needs in a much more careful way than in the past. In a certain sense, this should be approached in a customised manner, looking at internal and external resources, current and prospective needs, strategic independence, environmental impact, and of course costs of raw materials, production, acquisition, distribution and waste disposal. The current situation is very diverse, with changing sources of supply, as a result of political, financial, historical-geographical, cultural or crisis-related choices over the past decades.

Then there is the question of the costs of the energy sources included in the portfolios of the various states. Here, too, the issue is complex. We have said that there is a considerable difference between the cost of energy at the source and for the user. That is not all. The cost of oil or gas, for example, varies greatly as a result of the supply/demand relationship, due to deliberate political actions by producer countries, financial crises and conflicts. The same is partially true for other renewable sources, whose cost can vary with respect to weather and plant density: in the case presented above, too much sunshine in California reduces or even nullifies the price advantage of electricity from solar, making such systems less profitable and therefore more expensive. The cost of electricity also includes the financial return on investment to build the plants, through a parameter called LCOE (levelized cost of electricity). There is an inherent complexity in this type of estimate, due to costs that are not directly visible, the time required to build the production plants, the distribution and eventual storage of the energy, the costs of disposing of the plants and their different lifetimes, which are not always taken into account. Comparisons then become difficult and subject to great temporal and geographical variations.

An example is the current comparison between nuclear and renewable kilowatt-hours: nuclear provides energy that is now very expensive to produce - given the cost of today's infrastructure - but easy to distribute and always available, which is then remarkably cheap for users; for renewable, the exact opposite is true, because the system costs (distribution and storage) are indirect. For example, due to the impossibility of creating large storage facilities, renewable requires the daily capacity market payment of gas turbines that are normally switched off, but ready to go if the sun and thus the electricity is lacking. Very roughly, today's cost of a Megawatt-hour of electricity varies from a few tens of euros to hundreds of euros, depending on the energy source and the country. And, as mentioned earlier, the figures change significantly if we consider the cost of the associated infrastructure.

The total power produced in the world today is a huge number: about 4,000 billion watts - by way of example, an LED light bulb has an output of about ten watts. Remember that more than 50 per cent of this power is generated by fossil fuels (natural gas, oil and coal). This is followed by renewable energies such as solar, hydroelectric, wind and hydrogen. Nuclear power accounts for only 10 per cent. Similarly, we can express the energy needs (and consumption) of different countries in Mtoe: one Mtoe is the energy generated by one million tonnes of oil. China, at the top of the list, consumed a full 4,000 Mtoe in 2023, followed by the United States with about 2,200Mtoe. Assuming a barrel cost of USD 80, this leads to a total for our country of about USD 80 billion per year. Forecasts for 2050 foresee a substantial increase in demand and thus needed capacity. And because of plans for decarbonisation, for which 2050 will be a crucial date, the World Nuclear Association predicts that, as far as electricity is concerned, production will be almost completely decarbonised, with 67 per cent from renewables, 12 per cent from coal and 16 per cent from nuclear. Of course, the scenario could change depending on the success of the various research and development projects underway, particularly for next-generation nuclear power.

Fortunately, the price of the transition to low-carbon energy systems is much lower than perceived by society and than imagined by policy-makers. On the contrary, the cost that would be paid for any delay would be much higher, as critical energy systems are subject to the environmental, economic and social consequences of climate change, in a perverse feedback mechanism. Moreover, the various energy supply systems, which are at the heart of all the world's advanced economies, are not only extremely complex, but also highly interconnected. The need for decarbonisation therefore justifies a rapidly evolving technological scenario, largely determined by the search for economically, politically, ecologically and socially sustainable solutions. The choices that will be made will in turn impact downstream users, be they industrial infrastructures, civil installations or urban communities, which will need a very long time to adapt to these changes. The result is that, despite the availability of numerous alternatives to fossil fuels, bureaucratic-regulatory barriers and political vetoes often still prevent their large-scale use. Last but not least, the large availability of options on the table will make an *integrated approach* imperative, to build the optimal cocktail for each country.

The complexity of the green energy portfolio thus shifts directly to the base of the pyramid: to those infrastructures and systems (especially industrial ones) that are particularly energy-hungry (Figure 7).

Take the example of a large industry, be it a steel mill, a cement factory, a chemical company or a tile manufacturer. These factories simultaneously need electrical power and heat, the latter necessary to support a large number of ancillary industrial processes. A simplistic approach might be to purchase electricity and partially use it for heat production. This is, of course, a strategic and financial mistake, but also a "physicsmistake".

Figure 7   Total energy consumption by sector and source in 2023

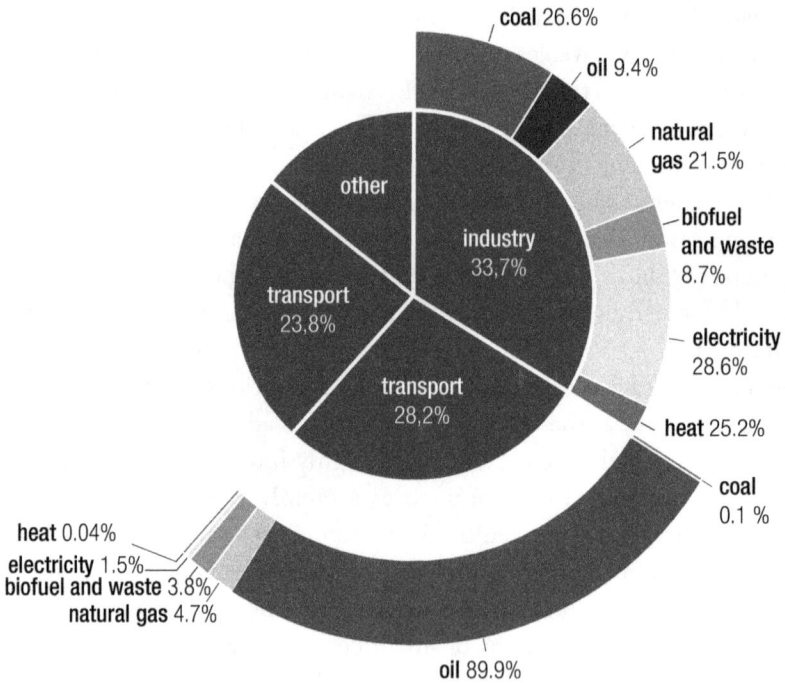

Source: revised based on UN Department of Economic and Social Affairs, *Energy Statistics Pocketbook* 2023, New York, 2023.

Electricity is energy in a particularly organised form, with energy stored and ready to change form for useful purposes, while heat is energy distributed in a disorganised form. In scientific terms, the electricity is said to be a low entropy energy, while heat is the highest entropy energy in nature. This consideration is directly reflected in the efficiency of energy use (and thus cost). One option would then be to have a turbine (*e.g.* a gas turbine) in place for the combined production of energy and heat (the latter a natural by-product of the operation of such a device); the cost of energy would be lower, as distribution costs would be zero.

At this point, however, the question of decarbonisation arises. Although to a lesser extent than oil or coal, burning natural gas also produces CO_2. The iron or cement produced by the industry would therefore not be green. To remedy this problem, the company could choose to generate electricity by using, for example, renewable source energy by placing wind turbines or photovoltaic installations on its territory. But these installations, on the one hand, require considerable space, and on the other hand, as we have already seen, are subject to large variations in production (*intermittency*), implying other notoriously complex and expensive infrastructures for storage and distribution. If the factory is located in a particularly windy or sunny area, the problem may be less relevant, but it is obvious that for effective industrial planning it is impossible to generalise or to submit to energy supply diktats. The solution, then, could be to install a small nuclear reactor on site and produce all the (green) energy and heat needed, without additional costs and with a very small 'energy footprint'; besides the fact that the foreseeable production surplus could be sold or donated to local communities near the plant. This is an option that deserves to be discussed in more detail.

It is no coincidence that the topic of nuclear power, closely linked to decarbonisation goals, was addressed in a 2022 UNECE (United Nations Economic Commission for Europe) report.[1] Although using 'diplomatic' language, being recommendations to sovereign countries with their own energy strategies, the report encouraged the various governments to address the issue of nuclear energy without prejudice. The UNECE notes that "for countries that *support* nuclear power, nuclear power generation can be a low-carbon source of energy and heat. In countries that *decide to*

---

[1] UNECE, *Annual Report 2022*, Geneva 2023.

use nuclear power, it can play an important role in decarbonising the energy system...". It is further stated that:

> ...policy-makers *interested in* increasing the deployment of nuclear reactors should consider designing, implementing and/or adopting policies, standards, legislation, incentives and/or programmes to *extend* the operating life of existing nuclear reactors, which are structurally safe, to improve the regional energy endowment... UNECE countries using energy from nuclei may wish to *reconsider* their current plans to close their nuclear power plants, to delay this process until the capacity of other low-carbon sources is sufficient to fully cover energy demand.

Furthermore, policy-makers should:

> accelerate the development and deployment of advanced nuclear technologies, including small modular reactors, to produce high temperature heat and hydrogen [...] and new nuclear power plants should be considered if safe and feasible. The new generation of small reactors, in particular, can be safer, cheaper and more efficient than conventional reactors. They could be implemented on a large scale to meet energy needs in places where renewables alone cannot meet demand.

In short, this is a message of encouragement, without prejudice to the decision-making independence of the different states.

To simplify, the concept expressed by the UNECE, addressed to our continent, is: "European governments, if you do not have strong political reasons not to do so, seriously consider incentivising nuclear power, with a view to complete decarbonisation in Europe". Implicit in this sentence is an exhortation to implement new models of public-private collaboration, following what is happening in other regions of the industrialised world.

5   Catamaran Elssa, Strait of Malacca

Renewables: Green and other Colours

The catamaran sails swiftly through the calm, turquoise waters of the strait, propelled by the force of the wind and waves. The sun shines high in the sky. The sails are stretched by the wind that blows constantly from the south-west, generating a force that is transferred to the catamaran through the rigging and boom. The waves, also created by the wind blowing across the surface of the water, add another level of motion: the boat rises and falls as the waves pass, with their energy absorbed and converted into motion. On the deck of the catamaran, we enjoy the ride. The helmsman uses the wind and waves in our favour, adjusting the sails and rudder to maintain an optimal course. The combination of wind and waves, both carriers of energy generated by the sun, creates a smooth and steady gait, allowing us to move efficiently through the waters of the strait. Indeed, the sun, the primary source of energy, heats the air and water, generating the temperature gradients that power the winds, that in turn agitate the sea surface, raising waves that travel thousands of kilometres.

Harnessing these natural energies, the catamaran moves without the need for engines, in a perfect combination of applied physics and engineering. We, on board, witness this natural balance. We feel the wind caressing our faces, listen to the rhythmic sound of the waves crashing against the hulls and watch the play of light and shadow created by the sun's rays on the water. But the poetic aspect of the situation hides the complexity of the physical phenomena behind it all and highlights two sources of 'clean' energy - or 'renewable' energy as they say nowadays - in the collective imagination and also in substance: solar and wind power. The catamaran harnesses both, thanks in part to a series of solar panels that provide electricity for the crew's essential needs. However, while for our boat there is a fine energy balance between nature and ecological sources, realistically this is unattainable for most other human activities, especially those related to heavy industry and commercial transport. On the other hand, we have seen that continuing as if nothing were happening - 'business as usual' - is impossible. A paradigm shift will be needed, and we will finally have to think about energy in an intelligent, conscious and non-predatory way, unlike what we have done so far.

Earth, wind and fire

We have already said that each country's energy portfolio must be diversified, but also contain components specific to its particular geographical, political, cultural and economic nature. The need for decarbonisation favours nuclear and renewable energies, which must be accompanied, although with a gradual reduction, by components that are not neutral from the standpoint of the climate crisis but cannot be eliminated immediately, such as oil and natural gas. Among renewables, two sources stand out as particularly promising solutions for the future, especially because, like nuclear fission and fusion, they are the subject of considerable research and development programmes and are interesting from the point of view of foreseeable technological improvements and cost reductions. We are talking about solar photovoltaics and hydrogen.

Solar energy today covers only 5 per cent of the world's energy needs; a small fraction but certainly destined to grow rapidly in the coming decades, thanks to the aforementioned advances in technology. A great advantage of the source is its intrinsic 'entropic' quality: the energy of the sun is directly converted into 'low-entropy' electrical energy, with no other waste than an incidental production of heat. Today, moreover, the solar field is in turmoil due to a series of very important and promising developments, in many ways revolutionising the renewables market.

First of all, solar panels are becoming continuously and permanently more efficient - a measure of how much electricity they produce for the same amount of sunlight. This is due to the use of innovative materials and new techniques in the construction of solar panels. In the same vein, 'two-sided' panels, *i.e.* where both sides of the devices are sensitive, produce a net increase in efficiency, consequently driving down the cost of the devices and the kilowatt-hour. In parallel, the use of a new generation of transparent solar panels will increasingly allow the surfaces of civil and industrial buildings to be exploited in addition to classic roofs (think of window coverings or other architectural structures).

Another aspect is the aforementioned intermittency of the energy source, which is increasingly mitigated by the development of new-generation battery-based storage systems.

The last point is the use of 'smart' panels, based on computerised management by artificial intelligence that, for the technical performance of the devices, allows efficiency gains based on the monitoring and optimisation of their operation. It is evident that by adding up the gains for each of the above points, the result is a substantial increase in the convenience of this important energy source.

As for more interesting technological developments, we note the widespread use of perovskite, named after the Russian mineralogist Lev Perovski. Normally, a photovoltaic panel contains a thin, light-sensitive layer of silicon; in the case of the most innovative devices, silicon is replaced by perovskite, a material that is also crystalline, but with intrinsically and better functional characteristics than silicon. Its use makes it possible to increase efficiency and reliability overall and to reduce the cost of panels. Added to this will be massive applications of large panels on water surfaces, which will decrease the amount of land occupied and increase efficiency through cooling by the water (the idea is to realise systems similar to those of wind turbine batteries installed offshore). The hope, finally, is that the disadvantages of solar energy - environmental impact, cost and complexity of disposal - can be resolved by the advancement of technological progress, in turn stimulated by an expanding market.

On the other hand, the use of hydrogen gas (H_2) is also a promising option for obtaining renewable and climate-neutral energy, both qualitatively and quantitatively. However, as we have already mentioned, hydrogen is an energy carrier rather than an actual source: while the sun, oil and uranium are for all intents and purposes directly usable resources for producing useful energy, hydrogen - like electricity - is rather a means of transporting or storing energy.

Since this gas is absent from our atmosphere but appears in the molecules of three relatively common substances in nature - water (H_2O), methane (CH_4) and ammonia (NH_3) - it is necessary to resort to complex techniques to extract it from these compounds and then use it for the purpose of electricity. It can, however, also be created from renewable energy sources such as solar or wind power, and very interestingly, as a by-product of the operation of a nuclear reactor.

Hydrogen is an inherently green element, and when used to operate a fuel cell, only generates water as a waste product. All these characteristics make it a viable solution for civil transport and electricity generation, but also for supplying energy to homes and many other applications that would otherwise make use of CO_2 generating sources. Essentially, hydrogen allows energy produced from other sources to be stored and converted efficiently, ensuring greater efficiency and flexibility in distribution networks.

Hydrogen fuel cells function like normal batteries but do not discharge or need recharging. They generate electricity and heat as long as the active element - hydrogen gas, in our case - is supplied. The device consists of two electrodes, one negative and one positive, embedded in an electrolytic substance. In a hydrogen fuel cell, a catalyst placed on the negative electrode separates the hydrogen molecules into protons and electrons, which take opposite paths due to their different electrical charges; the electrons pass through an external circuit, creating a flow of electricity, while the protons combine with oxygen to generate water and heat.

Much of the hydrogen produced in the world is used by the oil industry and for other chemical-industrial processes. In the future, though, the use of hydrogen is likely to become dominant in energy generation. Today, hydrogen cells are already being used to power the electrical systems of spacecraft, for various electronic devices, to provide electricity to remote locations not connected to power grids, and increasingly, to run civil transport vehicles. In fact, hydrogen is considered a promising substitute for petrol, due to the absence of greenhouse gas emissions. And a fuel cell can be several times more efficient than a petrol engine. Hydrogen can also be an effective high-temperature heat generator for industrial uses, a means of reducing the amount of iron needed for steel production, and a possible substitute for natural gas for domestic heating.

Today, many manufacturers of cars and public transport buses have adopted hydrogen. The main impediments to further expansion of the technology are cost and the difficulty of refuelling. Hydrogen recharging stations are similar to normal petrol pumps but, to give you an idea, there are currently only two hundred in all of Europe, which is why the spread of hydrogen vehicles is languishing. But this is a typical vicious circle that can become virtuous: with adequate investment in the sector, the cost of hydrogen and fuel cells can be reduced, making vehicles more affordable and encouraging the construction of widespread supply networks - a bit like what has happened with electric cars, for which charging stations have increased exponentially in recent years, growing in number as car prices have fallen.

For hydrogen, some safety problems certainly remain, but here as well, research is producing concrete results. For example, work is being done on using the gas - alone or in mixtures - in large power plants now running on natural gas turbines.

A problem we have already discussed for other energy sources is that of the type and amount of energy needed to produce hydrogen fuel cells: this energy must naturally be less than what will eventually be generated, and it must be green, otherwise we are producing climate-neutral energy... by burning fossil fuels. Based on these considerations, hydrogen on the market today has various 'colours' that specify its 'ecological footprint' (Table 1). This characterisation is interesting for our purposes because it shows us how careful we must be in the various transformations that a given energy source - green or otherwise - may undergo.

First, there is environmentally-friendly (green) hydrogen, produced by electrolysis of water using electricity from surplus renewable sources such as solar or wind power. Electrolysers use an electrochemical reaction to split water into its components (hydrogen and oxygen) without emitting any CO_2. Unfortunately, today green hydrogen is only a small percentage

Table 1   The different 'colours' of hydrogen, with their respective production processes

Colour	Source	Process	Products
Green	Electricity	Electrolysis	Hydrogen + water
Blue	Natural gas	Reforming	Hydrogen + CO_2
Black	Coal	Reforming	Hydrogen + CO_2
Pink	Nuclear reactor	Electrolysis	Hydrogen + water
White	Deposits	Extraction	Hydrogen
Grey	Natural gas	Reforming	Hydrogen + CO_2
Turquoise	Natural gas	Pyrolysis	Hydrogen + Carbon
Red	Nuclear reactor	Catalytic splitting	Hydrogen + water
Yellow	Solar energy	Electrolysis	Hydrogen + water

of the total, mainly due to economic issues. Blue hydrogen, on the other hand, is generated from natural gas, using a process (*reforming*) that combines it with water in the form of steam; unfortunately, CO_2 is also created with the hydrogen as a by-product. Black hydrogen, on the other hand, is by no means climate neutral, as it is produced using coal. In contrast, pink hydrogen, with no harmful emissions to the environment, is again created through electrolysis, but in this case powered by the energy of the atomic nucleus, which is also emission-free. The latest addition to the family, apart from other 'shades' under study, is white: this is a naturally-occurring hydrogen, not in the atmosphere but in underground deposits, apparently in large quantities. The main question will be how to extract it efficiently. Needless to say, this would be a very interesting green fuel, as it is available in nature without having to produce it by expending a lot of energy. It should be noted, however, that white hydrogen is not a renewable source, nor is nuclear power, which, however, as mentioned at the beginning, poses no stock-out problems.

As already mentioned, hydrogen is also an excellent method for storing energy in the case of intermittent production. Once it has been generated from any surplus energy from an irregular source, it can be stored in large natural caverns or depleted reservoirs, or on a smaller scale, in pressurised, fixed or portable tanks. In addition, hydrogen can be liquefied - and thus 'compacted' - and placed in cryogenic tanks for storage or to be used in liquid form in suitable engines. As with solar photovoltaics, the prospects for the future are very interesting, closely linked to the ongoing research and development activities in many countries around the world. The current problem, unfortunately, is the excessive cost of production. Perhaps optimistically, it is thought that hydrogen could generate a turnover of more than 500 billion euros by 2030; a very valuable investment option for future energy portfolios.

Finally, a note on ammonia. We have already observed that a molecule of this substance (NH_3) contains as many as three hydrogen atoms, combined with one nitrogen atom. Ammonia therefore has a very interesting chemical-physical property: it is the compound with the highest volumetric energy density among the various carbon-free hydrogen 'carriers'. It can be easily transported using the same transmission networks as liquefied hydrocarbons, such as propane, avoiding the construction of complex and expensive hydrogen pipelines; an alternative that is seeing considerable momentum and looks very attractive for the future.

The wind becomes more sustained, and so do the waves; here on the catamaran, the strong sensations increase. But let us not forget, with the somewhat cynical eyes of physicists, that waves and wind are nothing more than a way invented by nature to transport energy from one point to another...

6   *ENEA-Newcleo Research Centre in Brasimone, Tuscan-Emilian Apennines*

The Fourth Generation

In the United States, Idaho is now a new Silicon Valley for technology development and innovation in the field of nuclear energy. The US government has made available to the private nuclear industry not only tens of billions of dollars contributing to the development of new technology, with one dollar of subsidies for every dollar invested, but also land and scientific support from the Department of Energy. In China, similarly, a reactor is built every four months, and all kinds of innovative nuclear technology is supported and financed.

Fifteen countries in Europe are now willing to invest or reinvest in this field, and Italy too has created its own centre for the development of new fourth-generation nuclear reactors, here in the Tuscan-Emilian Apennines, through a public-private partnership on a technology that Italy has already been developing for almost thirty years, thanks to the impetus of then-ENEA president Carlo Rubbia: liquid lead for small fast reactors.

A small revolution is taking place in the field of nuclear power, as people are increasingly thinking about small, low-power devices, which are more versatile and safer than the large second- and third-generation plants currently in operation around the world. The relocation of nuclear energy sources is in fact following the path taken by other energy sources that, like nuclear, are aimed at achieving the complete decarbonisation of the planet.

Here at Brasimone there are many researchers. They are mostly young and from either engineering, computer science or physics backgrounds. Almost all of them have at least a non-specialist degree, a master's degree or a doctorate. For many of them, more than the realisation of the new generation of nuclear reactors, their work also has a social meaning: aspiring to achieve efficient, sustainable, affordable and safe energy for the future. After all, here, working on the new nuclear power is certainly synonymous with resourcefulness, intellectual curiosity and technological challenges, but it is also culturally concerned with the Earth and its energy for tomorrow, and beyond.

The centre is working on the qualification of components for the first commercial devices that should be produced within a few years. The (private) investments are considerable (several hundred million euros) and the patents obtained so far in the first three years of *new*cleo's life are numerous. From a certain point of view, this is very intensive research and development work, aimed at future production activity of an industrial nature. It is a gamble, after all, albeit one with relatively contained risks: you know what you want to achieve and you know how to do it, as there are no unknowns in basic science. And above all, there is a large market waiting. Everyone here says that the technical problems are there to be solved: the question is only how long it will take, and at what cost. Otherwise, one breathes the same air of freedom of research that exists among scientists at CERN.

Talking to Mariano, the manager of the centre, we learn that as part of the partnership with *new*cleo, the aim is to make two main products: a 200 MWe Small Modular Reactor (SMR) - a small lead-cooled fast reactor - and a 'closed' mini-reactor, a sort of large battery, of around 40 MWe, which, he proudly tells us, will be able to make a large ship, a small industry or a local community energy independent for ten to fifteen years, without any intervention, recharging or maintenance! But everyone's real 'fixation' is environmental sustainability. Mariano continually repeats that the energy produced with these devices is green, non-polluting and, above all, produced by safe and reliable devices, capable of democratising energy supply at low production and management costs compared to almost all other forms of green energy.

Above all, the most distinguishing aspect is a topic of absolute economic and social interest. Mariano explains that *new*cleo's devices plan to use the waste from current reactors of previous generations as fuel. They are therefore true 'nuclear scavengers', with the (not so) collateral objective of eliminating or at least greatly reducing the storage of radioactive waste. As they say, 'two birds with one stone'. The perspective is quite convincing, all things considered.

Our friend greets us with an invitation to attend the ceremony at the end of 2026 for the inauguration of the last plant to be built: an electric demonstration reactor, complete with all systems up to the turbine. For the real nuclear reactor, on the other hand, the regulatory path is at an advanced stage, and the invitation is for seven years from now in France. We save the date.

The state of the art

Data from the IAEA tell us that construction of more than thirty new nuclear power plants, mainly Russian and Chinese, has been underway around the world for some years now. These relatively conventional infrastructures will complement the other power plants built intensively in the 1970s, following the first oil crisis. Many of these reactors will be decommissioned in the coming years, once they reach the end of their nominal operating period - to date, around sixty to eighty years - exacerbating the energy supply problem. The IAEA again tells us that there are more than four hundred fission reactors worldwide, located mainly in Canada, China, South Korea, France, Japan, India, the United Kingdom, Russia, the United States and Ukraine (Figure 8). In addition to these are many reactors used for scientific research purposes, which are generally of limited power.

It may seem to be a contradiction, but even oil-producing countries such as the United Arab Emirates have recently embarked on a vigorous turn towards nuclear power, already covering 25 per cent of their needs in this way and aiming to reach 50 per cent. A recent IAEA report shows that since 2020, the number of newcomers to the club of countries interested in nuclear power has grown exponentially in just five years, now reaching over twenty-five new members.[1] This shows that the aversion to this technology is not generalised across the world, with an approach determined not only by emotional factors, but by financial and political ones as well. We can probably assume that those states whose economies are developing rapidly need energy *tout court* and are less sensitive to other considerations - just look at how dependent China and India still are on fossil fuels, despite the climate crisis (Figures 9 and 10).

Some might cite cultural and social reasons for these large differences: in some of the 'nuclear' countries, public awareness of safety issues, or of attention to environmental issues in general, might be lower or in any case depressed by economic 'blackmail'. From this point of view, it is no coincidence that it is precisely in Europe that the debate for/against nuclear power is most heated. Yet this, after all, also means that on our

---

[1] IAEA, *Small Modular Reactors. Advances in SMR Developments*, International Conference on Small Modular Reactors and Their Applications, 21-25 October 2024 (pdf available at www-pub.iaea.org).

Figure 8   Number of nuclear fission reactors in operation worldwide and percentage
of electricity produced by them

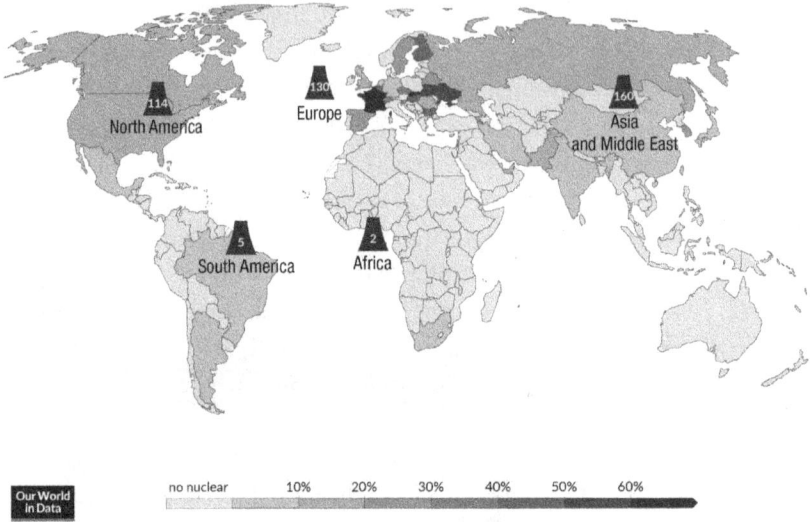

Source: Our World in Data (https://ourworldindata.org).

continent, and particularly in Italy, a serious and structured conversation
on the issue of energy can be undertaken. Moreover, the European Par-
liament itself has confirmed a truism, stating by majority vote that energy from the nucleus must be considered green, thus paving the way for
the inclusion of nuclear power - probably the fourth generation - in the
EU's future portfolio. This is supported by simultaneous funding for the
relevant research and development activities. This outcome is certainly a
compromise between the major European states, which are variously exposed to public opinion, fossil energy suppliers, and the different colours
of their respective governmental majorities. The different approach of
the governments of France (pro-nuclear) and Germany (relatively against)
stands out, for example, with equally diverse positions among the other
European partners.

The Russia-Ukraine conflict has undoubtedly contributed to this di-
chotomy. Notwithstanding the recent turmoil on the international stage,
Europe aims to eliminate its dependence on Russian energy resources

Figure 9   Share of electricity from fossil fuels in total electricity produced in 2023

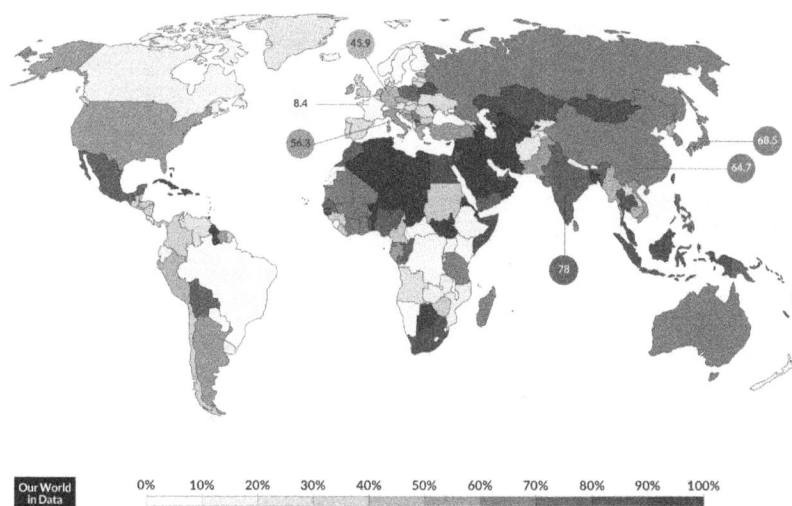

Source: Our World in Data (https://ourworldindata.org/grapher/share-electricity-fossil-fuels).

by 2027 and to continue on the virtuous path of decarbonisation. In this context, current and new nuclear power will have to play a role, along with the other green energies. Nuclear power's contribution to European electricity is around 25 per cent, with the ambition of an increase in the coming years. France generates more than 75% of its electricity from nuclear power plants, and given the investments made in recent decades, it is reasonable for the country to continue along this path in the future: fifty-six reactors in operation and six more in the pipeline, with an even more ambitious plan for future development to replace fossil sources. Germany, on the other hand, Europe's other major economic power, enjoys a small contribution from nuclear energy with only three reactors in operation; added to this are political and ideological reasons for favouring a drive towards renewables, while fossil fuels still continue to play a major role in the German portfolio, making it complex and probably financially costly to meet decarbonisation commitments. The message we take away is that since energy supply is a crucial issue for any country, and one that

Figure 10 Electricity produced in 2023 from renewables, nuclear and fossil fuels, in
absolute terms and as a percentage

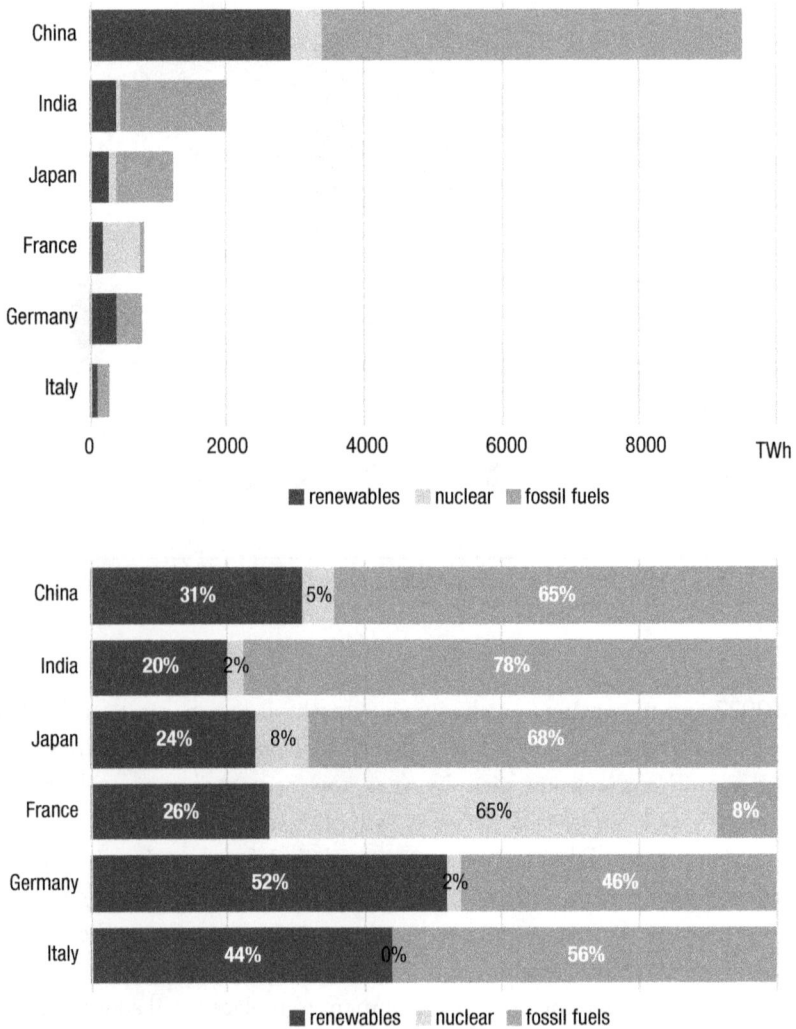

requires planning over the medium to long term, it is necessary that strategic choices, including towards nuclear power, have adequate guarantees
and be granted sufficient room to develop over time.

Small is beautiful

Considerable progress in the peaceful exploitation of energy from the nucleus has taken place in recent years under the influence of various scientific-technological and economic drives. The desire to overcome the problems of conventional nuclear reactors - cost, large size, slow construction, applications solely dedicated to electricity production - including those of the third generation, has led to the emergence of various designs for SMR (*small modular reactors*) and fourth-generation AMR (*advanced modular reactors*) (Figure 11). The latter are currently to be considered mostly at the conceptual design level (only a few are in basic/detail design phases) and will continue to be the subject of improvements and innovative solutions regarding both construction and operation.

In general, for both SMRs and AMRs, research is aimed at reducing radioactive waste, developing even safer machines - we speak of *intrinsic* or *passive safety* – that are reliable, socially and economically sustainable, and flexible in terms of their applications, which go beyond the simple production of electricity and concern, for example, the production of hydrogen,

Figure 11   Dimensions of the primary vessels of a small lead-cooled fast reactor, a large sodium fast reactor and a pressurised water reactor, and their power ratings

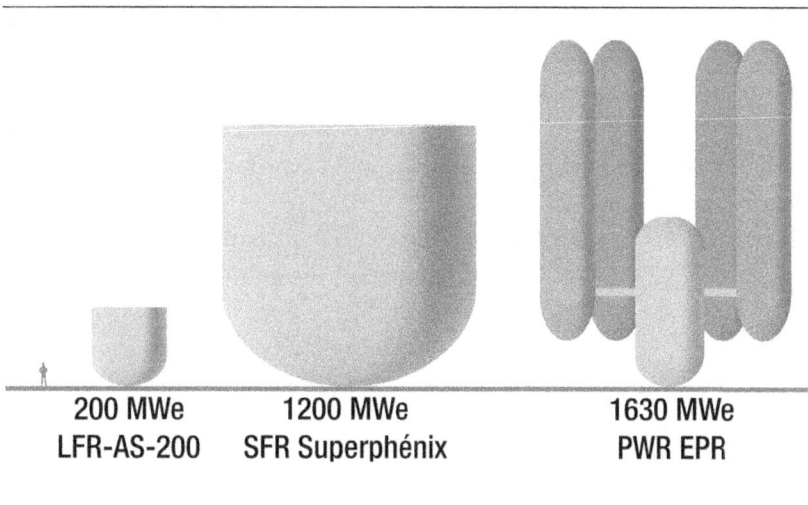

200 MWe	**1200 MWe**	**1630 MWe**
LFR-AS-200	**SFR Superphénix**	**PWR EPR**

and the creation of rare elements and high-temperature heat. Providing heat and electricity at the same time is a key factor in decarbonising the most energy-intensive sectors of industry, which today use gas turbines to produce the electricity and heat needed for their industrial processes. This, as mentioned, would be highly economically inefficient using renewables alone, not only because of the costs of storage and transport, but also because of the inefficiency of having to convert 'pure' energy such as electricity back into heat.

Already in a 2011 report by the American Academy of Arts and Sciences, Steve Goldberg and Bob Rosner identified a number of conditions that must be met for credible commercial fission development in the future.[2] First, given the massive contribution of industry and private finance, the cost of the nuclear kilowatt-hour must be low and competitive with other sources. This will allow for the arrival of significant private investments that can accelerate the energy transition. In addition, everyone demands that the new reactors be safe. This demand naturally imposes additional costs, unless the innovative design itself brings safety as a welcome side-effect; as we shall see, this is a paradigm followed for some of the technologies (but not all) of future fourth-generation devices.

Linked to the issue of safety, there is also the need to build plants that minimise the risks of nuclear proliferation, i.e. the misuse of reactor operating products for weapons purposes. Fortunately, nuclear plants are closely monitored by the IAEA through cameras, sensors and continuous infrastructure inspections, and attempts at military uses are impossible for a controlled civil plant. Then there is the issue of integrating the electricity generated by the new nuclear power with existing (and future) distribution networks: it makes a big difference, for example, to have many small reactors spread out over the territory instead of just a few large devices. Finally, there is the fuel operation cycle; with it come issues of safety, cost, and technological and political complexity that apply both at the start of the cycle (production of fissile material), during reactor operation (need for *refill*), and for waste disposal; short of recycling, as we shall see shortly.

At the beginning of the 2000s, an international commission that included Euratom (the European civil nuclear agency), France, Germany,

---

[2] https://www.amacad.org/publication/nuclear-reactors-generation-generation

Japan and the US Department of Energy (DoE), among others, set development priorities for so-called *Generation IV reactors*, identifying six technologies worthy of further study: gas-cooled fast reactors, molten-salt-cooled reactors, supercritical water-cooled reactors, liquid-sodium-cooled fast reactors, ultra-high temperature gas reactors and liquid-lead-cooled fast reactors. The primary aim was to design safer and less expensive infrastructures. For each of the techniques - which also differ in terms of the types of fissile material and the length of their fuel cycles - there has subsequently been considerable investment in research and development, both public and private, and everything suggests that some of these approaches will produce concrete results within a decade. Two sectors have been practically abandoned: gas-cooled fast reactors and supercritical water reactors, but the other four have given rise to numerous projects. As an aside, water in a supercritical state does not have a clear separation between the liquid and gas phase, increasing reactor efficiency and improving heat exchange. These reactors are similar to modern coal-fired thermal power plants with supercritical water, but with nuclear fission as the heat source.

The last category has some peculiar characteristics compared to the others, and therefore, we will use it as an example. Lead-cooled fast reactors, as already noted, allow for more efficient use of uranium through *reprocessing* of spent fuel. Lead-cooling also produces extra safety factors against hypothetical accidents, achieving the highest degree of *intrinsic safety*, and allows for the construction of reactors that are very compact and simple to build and operate, and therefore much cheaper. Finally, lead provides efficient *shielding* against gamma radiation generated in the core of the fissile fuel, which can be very useful in some cases.

These liquid lead-cooled small fast reactors can use MOX (*mixed uranium plutonium oxide*) as fuel, a name that conceals the concept of recycling existing waste for a new life as fissile material and the consequent mitigation of the issue of its storage: it indicates a mix of depleted uranium, a waste product of enriched uranium production, and plutonium, a by-product of reactor operation. This technology was born in the 1960s along with sodium-cooled reactors, devices which, as we have seen in the case of Superphénix, had high costs due to the management of the control of the chemical risk of this element that reacts violently upon contact with air and water. Modern molten lead modular reactors are offered in very small sizes (Figure 12). In practice, each of their parts can be manufactured in factories and transported already assembled without the need to be built at the future reactor site. We thus move from the more than 1500 MWe of the French reactor to devices of 30 to 200 MWe, with costs reduced by almost a quarter for the same power output. These new reactors are well suited to 'local' applications, for large industries or small communities.

For third-generation reactors, the production of fissile material is a laborious and expensive procedure. First the uranium is extracted, then it is enriched in the concentration of fissile isotopes. From this process, uranium-235 is obtained, while the 'depleted' uranium is stored in special storage centres spread over many nuclear sites. The operation of the reactor over long periods generates the fission products: many radioactive and non-radioactive elements, which are created by the splitting of uranium nuclei, and heavy elements, the most important of which is plutonium; these elements must also be disposed of. Furthermore, we observe that of the approximately two hundred tonnes of uranium that are extracted to make up the fuel needed for each year of operation of a typical reactor (1000 MWe), less than one tonne is used to actually produce energy; the rest contributes to the stockpiles in the repositories and is clearly an enormous waste of resources.

The principle of operating of a small modular reactor using MOX is drastically different to large-scale reactor operation. In this case, thanks to

Figure 12   Rendering of *new*cleo's LFR-AS-30 lead fast reactor, now in design and planned to operate by 2031 in France

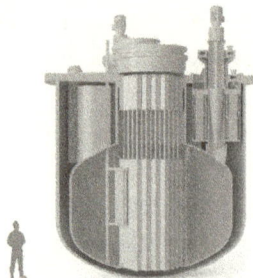

Source: www.newcleo.com

a reprocessing procedure - currently operating in only a few centres in the world - the waste is suitably treated to separate the material needed for fast reactors. These periodically generate more waste that is also reprocessed, in a circular and environmentally-friendly process. The result is that the volume and radiotoxicity of waste is reduced by orders of magnitude. A significant additional benefit of the use of a closed fuel cycle, fast reactors, MOX and reprocessing is the reduced need for waste storage sites, even taking into account their much lower radiotoxicity. If reprocessing becomes a widespread reality in European countries, a single storage site could be envisaged, capable of meeting the needs of all operating reactors for the entire continent. Finally, another environmental benefit would be the consequent reduction in the excavation of new uranium in old mines and the need to open new ones (Figure 13). It is somewhat surprising to think that the material already mined and the 'spent' fuel from European reactors, in a closed fuel cycle, could meet 100% of Europe's electricity needs for the next few hundred years. Our use of energy from the nucleus has so far been very inefficient!

Lead also offers considerable advantages for cooling. It melts at 327°C and boils at 1,737°C. In this very wide range, the metal is liquid and therefore very efficient at extracting heat from the reactor core, with large safety margins, making the possibility of coolant boiling - critical in conventional water-cooled reactors due to the potential risk of core meltdown - an impossibility. Reactor design is greatly simplified, reducing construction costs. Liquid lead also operates at atmospheric pressure, eliminating the need for thick containment walls (that, again, are expensive and cumbersome). Lead reactor operating temperatures can be much higher than those of water reactors, contributing to a higher electrical production efficiency (between 40 and 50 per cent), as well as the combined production of heat, which can be used for various purposes beyond what is required for the simple operation of the associated electric turbine. In the case of water reactors with a maximum temperature of 330°C, requiring a water pressure of 160 bar to maintain the liquid state, only about one third of the original energy is converted into electrical energy.

As we have said, small modular reactors, SMRs, are designed for industrial production and 'local' use. The IAEA defines 'small' as below 300 MWe and 'medium' as up to around 700 MWe. This definition is also espoused by the World Nuclear Association, which emphasises the simplicity of the designs, the possibility of mass production, and there-

Figure 13   'Closed' fuel cycle of a fourth-generation small fast reactor: enrichment
of waste and spent fuel from conventional (thermal) reactors can be used
to produce new fuel for fast reactors, which in turn can be recycled several
times.

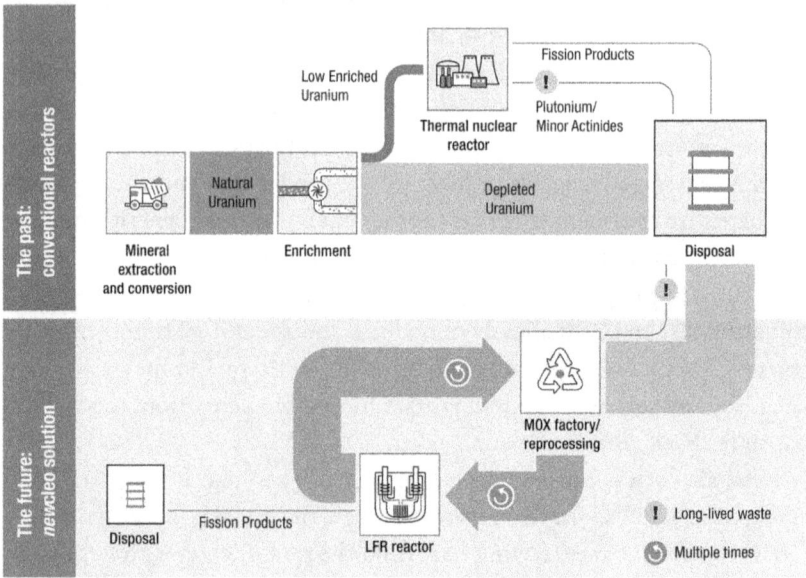

Source: www.newcleo.com

fore relatively short construction times and lower costs. Cost is obviously
a key driver for private companies, and SMRs can be inherently cheaper
than large conventional reactors for the same power output if they are
built and assembled following a standardized, or 'serial' process. Their
small size and possible passive safety features then make them suitable
for countries with limited distribution networks and limited experience
in nuclear power. Most SMRs are designed for a high level of intrinsic
safety in the event of a malfunction and can cope with natural events
(earthquakes or tsunamis) and deliberate or accidental attacks (terrorism
or human error, or aircraft crashes). Some are designed to be placed underground or underwater, some to be decommissioned coal-fired plant
sites, and others for on floating offshore platforms. The aim is to avoid
so-called exclusion zones and contingency planning, as the risk to the
population must be zero at the plant boundary.

As early as 2012, the DoE initiated contacts with various private companies for the development of small reactors, with the aim of having an in-house supply for the agency's purposes within ten to fifteen years. Public-private investment quickly reached the billion-dollar mark, to which was added another DoE grant for the study of micro reactors, with a capacity of less than 10 MWe. The public-private relationship has continued over the past decade with remarkable developments and initiatives on both sides. In the meantime, other international partners have adopted the US approach, following the Americans in the energy race for the future and also initiating advanced public-private synergy research and development projects.

Today, many private companies are involved in research projects in the field of SMRs in the US and other major industrialised countries, such as Canada, South Korea, Denmark, France, Japan and the UK, to name but the main ones, along with state-owned companies in China and Russia. The involvement of these new investors shows the profound change taking place in nuclear research and development: previously, these activities were led and financed by governments, whereas now they are increasingly managed by the private sector and by people with strong entrepreneurial goals, often linked to a social purpose, namely the dissemination of clean, cheap and CO_2-free energy. In this sense, the succession of private initiatives in the new nuclear sector is likely to make this energy source competitive with green renewable sources. This paradigm shift is similar to what we are witnessing in the exploitation of space, where private companies are conducting ambitious missions that only a decade ago would have been the monopoly of American, Russian, Chinese, Japanese, Indian or European public agencies.

Nevertheless, despite the very rapid technological progress of small fast reactors, there are many aspects that will need to be worked on over the next few years, especially with regard to the construction of prototypes of gradually increasing complexity. The time estimates depend on the particular approach taken by the various players involved in research and development. First of all, it must be said that considerable experience has already existed for years for small 'conventional' reactors. These are the hundreds of devices for naval military use - mainly aircraft carriers and submarines - with thermal power ratings of less than 200 MWt, which have been built and successfully operated for decades. They are generally small, pressurised water slow reactors, with significantly higher percentages of enriched uranium than those for civil use. In this scenario, Rosatom (a Russian state-owned company) is building a 300 MWe lead-cooled reactor that is expected to become operational as early as 2028, and on the same site it plans to recycle and produce MOX fuel. It should also be noted that, while conventional reactors in the past have taken, at best, between six and ten years to build and test - to which preparatory work on the design and permitting must be added - a small lead-cooled fast modular reactor would allow this period to be reduced to no more than three years for a full deployment phase.

Obviously, the financial aspect also plays a role: we would have to move from an overall cost of more than thirty billion euros for the construction of a large third-generation thermal reactor, with a construction time of around ten years, to a few hundred million for a fourth-generation fast reactor to be built in a few years and capable of operating stably and with few interventions for more than sixty years. This reduction in costs, investment value and construction time would increasingly open up the possibility of financing new installations through private capital.

The international situation is extremely dynamic and diverse. According to a 2024 report by the World Nuclear Association, around forty new water-cooled reactor projects, twenty high-temperature gas-cooled reactors, twenty innovative fast reactors - including molten-lead reactors - and fifteen molten-salt-cooled systems are registered worldwide, although many of these projects remain at the conceptual stage. The enormous technological, economic and political interest, coupled with the huge investments involved, bodes well for the achievement of practical solutions within a limited timeframe. Many organisations are active in advanced research and development programmes, some of which are already in the operational phase. Just to mention a few, the US company NuScale Power is planning to install more than fifty 840 MWe SMRs in twelve different modules in the near future; their closed-loop water-cooled system was the first to receive US federal approval. The ARC-100 reactor of Canada's ARC Clean Energy with a capacity of 100 MWe works with a very simple sodium-cooled uranium metal alloy, which consumes its own waste without leaving any slag. Then there are General Electric, X-Energy, Hyperion Power Generation, the now famous TerraPower (the company set up by Bill Gates that offers several versions of SMRs, including one under construction with liquid sodium), Japan's Hitachi, Terrestrial Energy, Westinghouse Electric, Sweden's Kärnfull Next and France's Nuward. Finally, there is the China National Nuclear Corporation, which will build the world's largest underground pressurised water reactor in a very few years.

In this 'ebullient' global context, Europe is advancing slowly with concrete and innovative projects such as the 30 MWe AMR reactor envisaged by *new*cleo, a company with an international portfolio founded on the basis of an Italian initiative and ideas, to be built in France, as it will be its first pilot plant for the production of MOX. The real risk that is foreshadowed is that the 5.0 energy race will play out between only a few countries - certainly the US - with determination, investment, attractiveness to experts and clear strategies, while other countries will stand by, engaged in endless discussions and debates on ideological issues. The winners, on the other hand, will determine the energy agenda - and consequently the economic agenda – for everyone else.

7 Paris, France (August 2050)

A Vehicle for Democracy

Jacques Lefèvre lives in Paris and works on artificial intelligence applied to fine arts at the Ministry of New Technologies, located in a skyscraper at La Défense. Each of his four working days a week, at least those for which he does not work remotely, unfolds according to a fairly usual routine. Jacques wakes up in his smart flat, designed to optimise energy efficiency and offer all services in a simple, reliable and automated manner. Home automation systems, controlled by artificial intelligence, in which he himself is an expert, automatically adjust the temperature and humidity of the rooms, the pantry and appliances, the lighting plan and even sleep and wake-up, thanks to the monitoring of Jacques' brain activity. The energy his apartment building uses is green and is produced by a nuclear battery, which also serves other neighbouring buildings. This source is complemented by new-generation solar systems integrated with the surfaces of the house. As is the norm, most residential buildings in Paris, as well as in other large European cities, are CO_2 neutral.

The self-driving metro that Jacques takes to get to work uses clean electricity, generated by the three fourth-generation mini nuclear reactors that power the Greater Paris urban area. Even the public buses, with hydrogen engines, are driverless. The rail and road transport networks are coordinated, managed by artificial intelligence that decides in real time the number and frequency of journeys according to demand.

Arriving at La Défense, we notice that the ministry building is a fine example of sustainable, green architecture, perfectly integrated into the surrounding vegetation and also CO_2-neutral. Jacques' team consists of a couple of human colleagues and a dozen virtual tutors and specialised androids. They are currently working on an interactive-immersive guide to the Palace of Versailles. Artificial intelligence and robotics are now a constant in the lives of most citizens in 2050. Success at work and social and economic well-being are now measured by the ability to manage and exploit these technological advances. A large part of manual and otherwise repetitive work is conducted automatically by automatons with artificial intelligence. People are employed in high-level creative or productive activities. After all, more than half of today's jobs did not even exist in 2025.

Work aside, leisure time is an integral and defining part of Jacques' life. Augmented reality takes centre stage, along with diversified and customised sports activities, and a healthy dose of human and family relationships. All this in a sustainable habitat, albeit massively supported by the most advanced technological developments, aimed at the physical and mental health of citizens and not just at economic profit. A dream comes true.

Visions of a possible future

When science-fiction books and films of the 1950s imagined the year 2000, they did so with a certain naivety, extrapolating incrementally from the scientific-technological knowledge of the time: gigantic computers, big missiles whizzing through the solar system, plastic clothes, freeze-dried food, you name it. But no internet, artificial intelligence, genetic engineering or mobile phones. Not for nothing did these developments represent completely unexpected and game-changing revolutions, certainly not the result of incremental or otherwise predictable development. Today, decades later, we can play the same game, already knowing, however, that the next unknown revolutions will once again make our predictions largely wrong. This is why it is wise to limit ourselves to projecting our knowledge to the 'near' horizon, a quarter century away at most. Nevertheless, since the current progress of science and technology is exponential, the coming twenty-five years are likely to bring many more unexpected results than the past twenty-five years, albeit in the hope that we will not have to experience global wars or cataclysms of various kinds that could slow down progress.

In order to imagine the world of 2050, it is imperative that we understand how the climate crisis - an unfortunate companion for humanity for several decades to come - will evolve. Consequently, we will have to foresee what strategies will have been implemented for decarbonisation, which in turn will be closely linked to the energy that will then be available. The climate crisis will therefore be a driver for much of human activity, at all levels. The most industrialised countries will have to implement global and shared strategies to halve CO_2 emissions into the atmosphere by 2030, to achieve neutrality in 2050, and to financially help developing countries. And we repeat, energy will be the main tool for solving the crisis, just as it was the main cause of it.

In this regard, by the middle of this century nuclear fusion will have been achieved, and the first test power plants will already be operational, although full commercial use will only be realised towards the end of the century. Oil and gas will still be used in the coming decades, but predominantly only in industrialising countries, while solar photovoltaics will have become very common and widespread everywhere, along with wind and hydrogen, thanks to new generations of devices based on developments in materials science. The real innovation, however, will be the safe and clean fission of which we have spoken extensively. It is foreseeable that the 'new nuclear' will not only constitute a substantial component of the world's 5.0 energy portfolio, but that its by-products and various applications, which we have covered in part and will return to in a moment, will usefully fill our lives in a safe, reliable and economical manner.

Thanks to artificial intelligence, electricity distribution networks will be complex and instantly optimised to avoid waste. The contribution of SMRs, distributed throughout the territory in a capillary manner and dynamically adapted to needs for the production of electricity for industrial and civil use, as well as heat for the various industrial processes and the heating of buildings, will be considerable. Land and sea transport, largely electrified and self-driving, will also make use of artificial intelligence. Large container ships and oil tankers, in particular, will have individual nuclear micro-reactors for their propulsion. Parallel developments in robotics and artificial intelligence will lead to an advanced generation of organic android-humanoids for industrial and domestic purposes, medical care or heavy-duty use.

As medical research advances, we also expect great progress in the life sciences. First, preventive health care will have become widespread, thanks to strong cultural awareness and the availability of advanced screening systems. The combination of innovative vaccine techniques, genetic engineering, immunotherapy, personalised medicine and future applications of nuclear physics in diagnostics and therapeutics (and other types of physics as well) will make it possible to efficiently treat cancer while respecting the patient's health and quality of life. We will have rapid and efficient tools to cope with the periodic attacks of new viruses and bacteria, which will become increasingly frequent due to mutations favoured by the climate crisis or the emergence of antibiotic-resistant bacterial strains. The average lifespan of human beings will leap considerably, as will the quality of life. The situation of global demography will then require special attention. The current plummeting birth rate in the most developed countries indicates that we will soon reach 'peak humanity', stabilising under nine billion people even before 2050. The side effect will be an ageing population, prone to new diseases that are currently unpredictable - not least because of the switching on of dormant genes for shorter average lives. This will necessitate new forms of care for old and very old age and the social reintegration of age groups now considered pensionable. Energy will also play a primary role here. The sustainable and fair distribution of energy is, as mentioned, a vehicle for democracy and will increasingly prove to be a necessary tool for reducing the disparities between the North and the South.

Small batteries

The Voyager 2 probe was launched on 20 August 1977, followed, in reverse order, by Voyager 1 on 5 September of the same year. For nearly fifty years, the probes have been travelling through space and to this day continue to send valuable data back to Earth, despite being far beyond the boundaries of our solar system. Admittedly, having been built in the 1970s, these probes have on-board electronics with millions of times less memory than a smartphone and transmit data tens of thousands of times slower than a modern Internet connection, but over the decades they have made a tangible contribution to our knowledge of the solar system. The on-board instrumentation includes various devices that consume just 250 watts: but where does the energy that has kept Voyager alive for half a century, and who knows how many more years, come from? Certainly not from solar panels, given the enormous distance from our star, nor from chemical batteries or fuel cells, which would have been too short-lived for the mission. The energy is produced by very special small batteries, which are still not dead after decades of incessant operation; these are nuclear batteries. They are likely to be the batteries of the future, destined to one day replace their electrochemical sisters in a myriad of applications, with efficiency, safety and, in perspective, low cost.

In the future, mini-nuclear batteries will be used for most electronic devices, first and foremost smartphones, or whatever they will become. Many people will have biomechanical supports to improve their quality of life and extend it: bionic organs, exoskeletons in the case of motor imped-iments, cardiac control systems and sensory aids; it will also be possible to power these devices with nuclear sources that will not need recharging.

But what is the principle behind these 'magic' batteries? We have seen that isotopes of heavy elements can emit radiation. Some of them, which are relatively stable and chemically non-reactive - *e.g.* corrosive or poi-sonous - can be used to build our nuclear batteries, which are particular-ly suitable for low-energy devices such as Voyager probes and our future mobile phones. Radioactive isotopes decay into alpha particles, electrons or gamma rays, according to the three known types of radiation. The first thing to reiterate is that heat, a form of energy, is generated in these re-actions. And if this heat is transformed into electrical energy, that's it: we have constructed a battery, an unconventional one, i.e. not based on electrochemical reactions, but for which the primary source of energy is the nucleus of a radioisotope.

The heat generated in nuclear decay reactions can be converted into an electric current using micro devices called *thermocouples*, albeit with relatively low efficiency. Another more efficient mechanism directly ex-ploits the production of the beta electrons generated in the decay: we then have so-called *beta-voltage* nuclear batteries. By converting a fraction of the energy of beta decay, these batteries can create a flow of electricity without relying on temperature differences. Direct conversion beta-voltaic batteries are among the most efficient on the market today. Then there are indirect conversion beta-voltaics, which use the light emission in the decay and a photovoltaic cell to produce electricity. What is interesting is that these radioisotopes are generally among the waste from the operation of nuclear reactors - a really good way to reuse them.

A further element characterising the quality of a nuclear battery is the 'lifetime' of the radioisotope. We speak in this case of *half-life*, i.e. the time after which a certain amount of radioactive substance is reduced by half. Since this time may be very long, and since we have an immense number of atoms within even a few grams of the substance, we understand that the life of our battery can be very long. Researchers have recently announced the creation of prototypes of beta-voltaic batteries based on carbon-14 (known for its use in dating methods for archaeological finds) for which the half-life is an astronomical 5,700 years, sufficient for the most ambitious uses. Another widely used element is the aforementioned tritium. Although it has a half-life of only twelve years, it is considered relatively practical, much more so than many other elements. When it decays, tritium emits beta electrons that can be shielded with thicknesses of less than a millimetre to protect human users. But the zoology of nuclear batteries does not stop at these examples, and there are - and will be more and more - applications that will help change our lives: security devices, low-energy systems (such as sensors), encryption and protection of sensitive data, and medical, military, space or underwater applications.

At this point, however, the usual irrational fear of radiation kicks in, and many consider it better to rely on electrochemical batteries, albeit with poorer performance. In this regard, the reality is the diametrical opposite. Modern chemical lithium batteries, for example, pose a number of risks. We have all been forced to switch our mobile phone off some times because it has overheated. In more serious cases, batteries can catch fire or even explode, perhaps generating fires that are very difficult to extinguish. This is the reason why batteries can no longer be carried in aeroplane cargo holds: a fire triggered by a battery's lithium could end tragically if left unchecked. In contrast, nuclear batteries would have no chemical or even radiological hazards, the source inside being duly shielded by the device's sealed casing, and in any event, the radiation levels absorbed in the event of deliberate misuse would be negligible.

The real limitation to the mass application of nuclear batteries currently is their cost. Radioisotopes can be rare and the technology required to use them expensive. However, even now, elements such as tritium appear cost-effective for most applications due to the possibility of using the batteries for very long periods, compared to lithium batteries. Some very promising studies conducted in China, the US and Europe foresee the use of nickel-63 for the construction of micro beta-voltage batteries, smaller than a coin and with a lifetime of more than fifty years, with no maintenance required. After fifty years of operation, a nickel-63 battery would still be able to produce 75 per cent of its initial power - ideal for mobile phones, drones, pacemakers or other low-power devices. Miniaturisation is undoubtedly the most interesting result of such revolutionary devices, the result of the major developments in nanomaterials in recent years. These new batteries generate a respectable level of power - one watt is thought to be reached in a very short time. Imagine never having to recharge your mobile phone or having a drone that flies for years without stopping! Moreover, their safety is of the highest level: they cannot catch fire or explode, as they can work well between -60 and +120°C, and without radiation passing through their sealed casing. Finally, these batteries are also environmentally friendly, as at the end of their life the initially radioactive substance is transformed into copper, which is non-radioactive and non-polluting. The question then becomes whether ideological or 'gut feeling' opposition will prevail despite the large number of benefits and convenience of such devices: the answer is probably - and fortunately - no. Meanwhile, research in the field is galloping forward, and we will soon see disruptive developments.

Large batteries

The real complexity of a nuclear power plant essentially relates to what lies outside the reactor. A complexity brought about by the requirement to have a safe, efficient and reliable plant, capable of operating for around a hundred years, and which must therefore be supplied with 'fresh' fuel periodically, say every five to ten years. We have already noted that used fuel, which is still radioactive, must be carefully removed, transported and stored in special containers for even very long periods. A similar approach applies to replacement fuel, which requires complicated and costly systems for management and logistics, which can account for up to 10-20 per cent of the cost of the energy produced, especially for mobile reactors, to be used on board aircraft carriers or submarines, for example. This complexity, which is acceptable for military purposes, would make it uneconomical to use for civil transport or other small- and medium-scale applications. The ideal, then, would be to have a standardised, simple, compact and easily and safely transportable system that would be used and then decommissioned, without the need for any recharging, and as such be operational for a relatively short period of ten to fifteen years. A kind of mega nuclear battery, but with great power.

If we reflect on the SMR revolution, we find ourselves in the same situation as when, in the 1970s, we experienced the end of the large mainframe computers, that were larger and more and more powerful, until the small microprocessor and personal computers arrived, leading to the concept of distributed computing power among many small units. Today we may be close to a similar paradigm shift for nuclear energy: the new generation of SMRs, relatively small and cheap reactors built in a serial manner, designed for very local, safe and simplified operation. In fact, the prospects are even better: the idea of designing even more simplified versions of SMRs, for which the idea of 'refuelling' the reactor is abandoned, effectively creating mega nuclear batteries, is becoming realistic. These systems could provide heat for industrial processes or electricity for a big city district, run for two or three decades and then be transported to the factory that produced them (serially) for refuelling and regeneration.

SMRs are designed for power outputs of a few hundred MWe, certainly much smaller than third-generation reactors, but still requiring factory assembly and appropriate installation at the site of operation. *Reactor batteries*, on the other hand, will have a very limited power output, up to around 40-50 MWe - enough to supply energy to more than thirty thousand flats - such that they would be remarkably simple to construct: a simple assembly line would be needed for an external container of the conventional reactor, small in size, and in some cases capable of fitting into a container for logistics. In addition, ancillary heat would be used to heat homes. The economic advantages of such an approach are obvious. A 40 MWe battery could cost 150-250 million euros when fully operational: this is equivalent to the fuel consumption of several years of a large commercial ship that needs this much power. The investment would also pay for itself quickly due to the absence of refuelling, the possibility of transporting more goods - thanks to the absence of tanks and the weight of fuel - and in less time. The argument is similar for economically and logistically disadvantaged communities not connected to large distribution networks, such as mining areas or islands. In addition, the installation of reactor batteries does not involve the complex construction sites that have posed significant and sometimes unpredictable problems for conventional reactors in the past, with considerable cost overruns compared to initial financial estimates. The reactor battery, on the other hand, is built and installed quickly and becomes a power source on demand, like a normal electric battery; a product like any other, not a large infrastructure, just like a personal computer compared to a large mainframe. Even from an environmental point of view, a nuclear battery would have a very small 'footprint' compared to a wind or photovoltaic plant with the same power output.

The numbers associating poverty with the need for energy are impressive: at least 1,000 kilowatt (kWh) hours of energy must be provided annually to lift a person out of poverty,[1] compared to the approximately 3,000 kWh consumed in the richest countries. This requires, for a near future humanity of almost ten billion people, the availability of some 30-40 trillion kilowatt hour, plus climate neutrality, making the use of nuclear power or nuclear reactor batteries an essential ingredient in solving the problem. In short, the combination of SMRs and batteries will certainly be a winning strategy towards the democratisation of green energy distribution for decades to come.

Finally, on the question of safety and how this is perceived by the public, ballast batteries are extremely robust devices by construction, one of their strengths. Their small size contributes to this characteristic. First, the amount of residual heat that has to be removed when the reactor is switched off is small. In addition, the core has a small volume relative to its surface area, making it thermally easier to cool without any external intervention. The system is essentially in equilibrium and is self-regulating. The reactor also has a compact and strong steel containment structure that completely surrounds it, passively preventing the release of radioactivity into the environment. The core module has smaller modules inside and only one of these, the control module, is accessible to operators; the other parts of the structure are factory sealed, with the fuel core already integrated. Nuclear power also allows devices to be placed underground to provide an additional level of protection against natural or deliberate external events.

Again, the research and development process is very advanced in the world. The train has left the station, and it will be difficult (and counterproductive) to stop it. The initial investment by private individuals is also sustainable, and certainly not comparable with the considerable (mostly public) funds needed for large infrastructures in the past, also considering the very short time between the design phase and the commercial exploitation of the battery. Many international companies are expected to produce results already in the next few years, with a number of pilot plants

---

[1] https://energyalliance.org/powering-people-planet-2023/the-global-challenge/

ready to be installed and put into operation in various countries around the
world. It will be important to communicate about the inherent safety of
these plants, but it will be very important to arrive at a low kilowatt-hour
cost in order to make the intrinsic 'green' nature of the energy produced
prevail.

Radiation against cancer

A final notable example is the use of atomic energy in the medical field,
a true revolution that has been consolidated over the last few decades and
that portends developments that were unthinkable in the past. Thanks to
these technologies, doctors and patients can tackle serious illnesses with
more powerful and effective tools, increasing the possibility of early diagnosis and successful treatment, even in situations where traditional medical therapies or surgery might not be sufficient. The methods are reliable,
safe and in continuous development, and exploit the results of research in
the field of medical physics being conducted in major international laboratories and large private companies. On the other hand, it is obviously a
big business, with a large number of companies involved and substantial
funding.

We have said many times that in much of society the subject of civil
nuclear power immediately evokes concerns about safety and risks - to
put it mildly - harking back to catastrophic accidents and unseen dangers,
sometimes falling into the trap of fake news and comments such as 'A
well-informed person told me that...'. We know that most of these fears
are unfounded, but it matters little. What matters is often the narrative,
regardless of whether it is genuinely related to correct information or art-
fully generated for other purposes. It is incontrovertible, though, that science and technology, in parallel with the 'energy' applications of nuclear
power described above, have favoured the use of energy from the nucleus
for medical applications, almost immediately after the first scientific discoveries in the field, with the aim of saving lives.

In 1896, the French physician Victor Despeignes began using radiotherapy, irradiating stomach cancer patients with the *X-rays* that had been
discovered by physicist Wilhelm Röntgen only a year earlier. Despeignes
determined that the disease regressed, and that the patients' pain was re-
lieved. Since those pioneering studies, the last century has seen a succes-

sion of applications of radiation for medical purposes. The net result is that several million people have been saved by therapies based on radiation applications. In this regard, it should be noted that bringing up such 'virtuous' examples is not an ex officio defence of nuclear power, wrongly considered by some to be 'all in all dangerous and perhaps unnecessary and costly', but an invitation to think critically and quantitatively about issues that are often approached superficially and with prejudice. Moreover, many of these medical applications of radioactivity are not always well known, beyond the normal X-rays that we have all experienced at least once. Yet, many developments in recent decades have opened up innovative strategies for diagnosis and treatment, such as modern versions of radiotherapy, which for many years now has been used to treat tumours using highly energetic gamma rays, protons and other electrically charged particles.

It is undeniable that oncology benefits greatly from the ability of the three types of radiation - alpha, beta and gamma - to deliver energy deep into cellular tissues, particularly cancerous ones. But at the same time, radioactive tracers are cunningly used as Trojan horses to highlight even microscopic lesions. In this case, we are talking about PET (positron emission tomography) - which exploits even the annihilation of matter and antimatter in the body - and SPECT (single-photon emission tomography). The former is particularly useful for neoplasms or early diagnosis of neurodegenerative diseases and cardiac perfusion, and the latter, for example, for functional imaging of the circulatory, cardiac and endocrine systems.

A fairly recent application worth mentioning is *proton therapy*, which uses protons to kill cancer cells, while at the same time managing to spare healthy ones, thanks to the specific physical properties of proton radiation. In proton therapy, the doctor uses a particle accelerator to energise the particles before they are directed at the tumour with great precision. Protons damage the DNA of cancer cells, killing them or preventing their uncontrolled reproduction, and fortunately, the DNA of cancer cells is particularly vulnerable because of their high capacity for division and limited ability to repair genetic damage. The great advantage of proton therapy over conventional radiotherapy is that this radiation adapts to the shape and depth of the tumour and spares much of the surrounding healthy tissues, preventing secondary diseases. Indeed, protons of a given energy have a certain depth of penetration and very few propagate beyond the

desired distance: the higher the energy, the greater the depth of interaction. It is therefore understood that treating an ocular melanoma with
protons means that the optic nerve downstream of the eye can be spared.
This technique, thanks to the expertise of nuclear, particle and accelerator
physicists, is increasingly being developed around the world, with infrastructures seeing the light of day in many large international hospitals.
This is certainly not the final solution, but a further 'peaceful weapon' to
be used in the medical arsenal.

Then there is *theranostics*, a neologism combining therapy and diagnostics. In a conventional PET scan, particular radioactive isotopes can
be injected into the patient together with a sugar solution. A tumour lesion, which is very energetic, tends to assimilate the sugar and with it
the isotope; therefore, the products of its decay can be detected by special
devices placed around the patient's body, typical of the tool bag of nuclear
physicists. At this point, the surgeon or oncologist has an accurate location
of the tumour and can decide on the best treatment strategy. The inge-
nuity of scientists goes further, however. The 'sentinel' isotope can also
be 'weaponised': special elements can be used which, once phagocytosed
by the tumour, also emit radiation that is harmful to it and not only able
to identify it. The advantage is considerable: radioactive damage occurs
in situ right in the tumour. It seems like the obvious solution: the lesion
is identified and irradiated at the same time, with the aim of killing the
malignant cells.

Finally, we cite the example of another variant of radiotherapy, *metabolic
radiotherapy*, an innovative therapeutic tool that is proving very useful in
the war against cancer. It involves the oral or intravenous administration
of particular radioactive elements to the cancer patient, which interact
metabolically with the tumour, producing 'selective' damage to it. Incidentally, this method will benefit greatly precisely from those radioactive
'waste' products resulting from the operation of fourth-generation mini
nuclear reactors.

In conclusion, the question of the implications of the use of energy from
the nucleus and its applications is primarily scientific and quantitative, and
certainly not debatable on psychological or ideological grounds. Understanding it requires a little effort, patience and knowledge, albeit not fully
accurate knowledge of how matter behaves in the depths of the atomic
and subatomic microcosm. The other aspect to consider is that the understanding of the biological mechanisms of radiation is progressing on a par

with the scientific knowledge of nuclear technologies. This should reassure us and help remove the aura of mystery and fear that surrounds the subject. We have the right to distrust people, but we should certainly put our faith in science, if only because of how it has improved our lives over the last four hundred years. Today we die far less from influenza or measles, we live longer, and the quality of human life is on average immensely better than it was only a century ago.

In short, nuclear and particle physics offers a wealth of high technology that can save hundreds of thousands of lives with the same technologies used to generate the nuclear energy that allows homes to be heated and industries to function.

Jacques, on a hydrogen-powered bus on his way home - where he will continue his working day - observes the skyline of his Paris silhouetted against the blue sky and thinks about how lucky he is to live right there and then, in a solid present that had been a possible future and will soon become a distant past.

At the same time, in Riau, on Indonesia's Mesanak Island, the storm has just passed and on board *Elssa 3*, the world's first catamaran for which the use of liquid fuels has been replaced by nuclear batteries, an aperitif is being prepared as the sun sets against a sky still strewn with many clouds. Antonio is now used to the routine on board. He embarked in Komodo and has already travelled more than a thousand miles to Singapore, where he and Stefano will participate in the seventh international conference on the use of nuclear batteries for naval applications, and where *Elssa 3* will be shown for the first time in the dock of the Republic of Singapore Yacht Club, right in front of the conference hotel.

"I honestly wouldn't have believed it if I hadn't had the experience first-hand," Antonio remarks, holding a glass of gin and tonic made from bottles bought in Australia. "It's really amazing to be on a craft whose only noise is that of the wind and waves on the hull, but with all the comforts of a luxury yacht, even air conditioning!"

"Yes, for the moment we are letting it go at full power", Stefano reiterates. "In this test phase I don't want to let the nuclear batteries get too hot. We keep the electricity consumption high during the day, thanks to the contribution of the photovoltaic cells; at night, when solar doesn't contribute, we'll keep the air conditioning to a minimum. Anyway, I'm really satisfied: after thirty thousand miles at sea, we've hardly had any problems yet. I've really realised my dream of a completely energy-independent, fossil fuel-free boat".

Antonio nods, while Stefano starts digging into his memory.

"Do you remember that with my first *Elssa* I was really set on being as energetically autonomous as possible? When during the Covid crisis I left for the round-the-world voyage, there was the fear of not being able to rely on supplies. I had covered the deckhouse with solar cells and installed two independent hydro-generators; wind turbines were noisy and inefficient, so I no longer considered them. I wanted to install electric motors, but in the end the technology was too immature, and fortunately, they didn't let me do it. I could only recharge the batteries when sailing at high speed and in bright sunshine; otherwise, I always needed to switch on the diesel generator. Then, after five years, the hydrogenerators had broken down and were inadequate anyway, the solar cells had become very inefficient due to the deterioration caused by the sun's radiation, and my generator hours had become too long."

"And then *Elssa 2* arrived...," whispers Antonio while sipping his cocktail and offering an assist to Stefano to continue his narration.

"Yes, there I put the experience gained from the first round-the-world voyage to good use, but I still couldn't completely renounce fossil fuels. I installed an electric motor for each hull and a dedicated diesel generator, then literally covered the deckhouse and also the side hulls with solar cells. Motor navigation became quieter and the boat, lighter and simpler, also consumed less, even though it was longer. However, the cost of maintaining the solar cells over the years was exorbitant, but when sailing I practically never used the generators, thanks to the recharging efficiency of the electric motor's propellers under sails, and the consumption of diesel fuel was reduced very significantly. However, I never trusted lithium batteries at sea and every eight years I changed them all to avoid the risk of fire or an explosion on board; an economic drain, given the amount of storage needed, and then it was really bad for the environment. In the end, the running cost during my second round-the-world voyage was more significant than that of the first *Elssa*, but I got more satisfaction".

Antonio thinks back to the long road travelled, not to *Elssa 3*, but the long and winding road that led to today's technological developments, while Stefano continues with his story, which his friend knows well. But the situation, the wind and the sea, stimulate the memories.

"The idea of nuclear batteries has been an obsession of mine for as long as I can remember, but in the early years of *new*cleo we didn't have time to develop the concept. However, when we built the first fourth-generation liquid lead reactor in France, we were already thinking about the fact that the radioisotope industry for medical and energy use would sooner or later explode, so we designed our fuel with great activation capabilities for nuclear battery material".

"And don't forget the reuse of waste!"

"How could I! We also investigated the recycling of fission fragments, and this was a great help. Thanks to those developments, we were able to make an initial strategic agreement with the Chinese for the production of nickel-63 smartphone batteries, and then, on the basis of the excellent collaboration set in motion, we obtained an exclusive licence with the European Union for power battery technology. In fact, at the beginning of *new*cleo I never thought I would become a licensee of Chinese technology because we were already negotiating to offer them a licence on liquid lead technology for nuclear reactors in 2020. But I am happy with that; they grew a lot as we launched the first fleet of advanced modular liquid lead reactors.

"And now you have the world exclusive on marine applications!"

"With this test world tour, we have gained experience and applied new ideas. I believe that the licence can become a partnership for future versions. On *Elssa 3* we still have the storage batteries to balance all the energy inputs from the three sources - solar, hydro-generators on the electric motor blades, and the nuclear batteries - but if in the future we manage to increase the power of the batteries, we can even use just those!"

Antonio interrupts: "Yes, but we know that the optimal solution for the energy supply, whether of a boat or an entire country, is usually more complex, and a mix of different energy sources leads to optimisation of systems and costs".

"True, but think that if the fear of nuclear power, which had been inculcated in us since the Cold War, had not disappeared, we could never have reached the Net Zero CO_2 target for this year; we are almost there now and on our way to reversing our greenhouse gas production. And thankfully so! Navigating is increasingly difficult with these extreme weather events".

"Do you remember when we talked about it at CERN's Cantine at Carlo's [Rubbia, -*Ed*] 90th birthday party? Did you ever think it would all go so fast?" says Antonio.

Stefano resumes his story, as the sky, just a few miles north of the equator, lights up with wonderful colours: "I can't believe it all happened so fast, after twenty-five years of waiting since I started working on this technology in 1994! The world really changed in 2021, first because of the strong push to decarbonise electricity and energy production, then because of the war in Ukraine, which prompted Europe to look for a truly independent and programmable energy source. It was a bit difficult at first, because investors and industrialists had by then created a narrative about renewables that allowed them extraordinary leverage on public monies, and they didn't like the sound of any serious competition for access to European or government funds at all.

"Well, the key was to transform the nuclear industry from public management to private initiative and to show that a new industrial approach could create truly economically competitive production", says Stefano.

"It was clear from the beginning: the agility of the private sector allowed for fast innovation, enhanced efficiency in project implementation and cost management, and the possibility to freely choose a winning long-term industrial strategy. The idea of using nuclear waste as fuel completed the picture of success, because the electricity sales of the first fourth-generation power generation machines were complemented by the earnings from waste recycling, which allowed us to create an extraordinary industrial supply chain. Combined electricity/heat cycles were the first to economically beat fossil fuels and allowed the production of hydrogen and sustainable liquid fuels and the decarbonisation of energy-intensive industrial processes: steel production, chemicals, ceramics and so on".

"Certainly, significant help came from the need to counteract the climate crisis", Antonio concludes.

"When we put the first reactor on a commercial container ship, it was clear that nuclear power was the missing link in the fight against climate change, and the idea of putting reactors on floating platforms made it possible to support the decarbonisation process, making it easier for the so-called developing countries to generate electricity independent of fossil fuels. People have gained confidence in technology, and in particular in nuclear power. We have begun to make the most out of the 'treasure' represented by fission fragments and extract the components for mobile phone batteries, then for pacemakers, exoskeletons and a host of medical devices".

"I am convinced that this is just the tip of the iceberg: think of how many applications there will be for mini batteries, that are as of yet unimaginable! In any case, what a beauty to never have to recharge your mobile phone..."

"A future yet to be written but remember how much we fought to get the use of radioisotopes for therapy into the pharmacy with our AAA[2]?" interjected Maribel, Stefano's wife, who in the meantime had joined the aperitif after the last swim of the day. "At a time when nuclear power for electricity generation was almost a taboo, we managed to achieve a powerful entry into the world of oncology, with a very successful therapy in the field of neuroendocrine tumours, and today the most succes-

---

[2] Advanced Accelerator Applications, a French-based pharmaceutical group specialising in diagnostics and therapy in nuclear medicine. The company, founded in 2002 by Stefano, was acquired in 2018 by Novartis, which then sold the diagnostics division to Siemens Healthineers in 2024.

sful oncology products are based on nuclear-produced radioisotopes, the first line in almost all anti-cancer therapies!"

"We are at version 2.0 of Prometheus!" exclaims Antonio. "He got fire from the gods: chemical energy that greatly advanced the human being, but only up to a certain point. Energy that could create destruction but also generate an infinity of applications. And today, the same is happening with energy from the nucleus. At the risk of being rhetorical, it is a new era of progress".

"In fact, all that is missing now is the widespread use of fusion", says Stefano. "But we are close there too. There has been so much progress lately; the problem has remained the cost. Sooner or later we will find the game-changing application that will launch it, perhaps for space exploration, for which it could be an indispensable tool. Sure, we have gas reactors on the moon base and the orbiting space station, but can you imagine how much propulsive energy we will obtain when we can eject plasma at fusion temperature through the nozzle of a rocket? The Mars base would become a reality, now that we are certain that there is underground water there!"

"These thirty years of technological development have felt like a new gold rush! The race for inexhaustible, green, safe and cheap energy, which has ignited new dreams and fantasies for a future of mankind yet to be written," says Antonio with deliberate emphasis as his mobile phone rings. Paola, his wife, cools him down. She advises him not to overdo it on board, reminding him that he is still a half-bionic old man and that he also suffers from seasickness...

Acknowledgements

Antonio and Stefano would like to thank Rebecca Servadio and Alessia Uslenghi for trusting their small project, and are grateful to Gabriella Buono, Safiria Buono, Ruggero Corrias, Giulia De Benedetti, Arianna Farinelli, Paola Scampoli, Maribel Lopera Sierra, Violetta Toto and Vittorio Vaiarelli for their contributions and critical reading of the manuscript.

The Authors

Stefano Buono

Stefano studied in Turin, where he graduated in Physics in 1991. As early as January 1990 he worked at CERN, a centre he would not leave for the next thirteen years. In 1993, the Director General, Nobel Laureate Carlo Rubbia, announced the project to produce safe, clean and sustainable nuclear energy, an idea that Stefano would embrace for life. In the feverish work of the 1990s, he realised how energy from the nucleus could be safe and sustainable, but also 'useful' in other fields, such as medicine, and in 2002 he founded Advanced Accelerator Applications (AAA), which exploits nuclear physics to successfully diagnose and treat certain forms of cancer, accelerating the development of a branch of medicine that is now booming. After listing AAA on the Nasdaq in 2015 and selling it in 2018 to Novartis, Stefano focused on facilitating the energy transition with a new generation of reactors that are completely safe, economically very competitive and that burn the radioactive waste produced by the traditional nuclear industry, guaranteeing energy for hundreds of years, even from this already existing material. And he decided to do so once again through a 'private' initiative to ensure speed, foresight and efficiency for the project, by founding *new*cleo.

Antonio Ereditato

Antonio studied in Naples, where he graduated in Physics in 1981 and where he later also received his PhD in 1987. Fresh from his degree, he joined CERN, where he stayed for many years working on experiments to study elementary particle physics. After holding a position at the National Institute of Nuclear Physics, he became director of the High Energy Physics Laboratory at the University of Bern in 2006. There, along with research activities in the field of particle physics and its technological applications, and assignments in science policy, he discovered a passion for training young researchers. At the same time, he undertook intensive work in the field of popularising science, including writing numerous essays aimed at a wide audience, which have been translated into several languages. The author of more than 1,500 scientific publications, in 2015 Antonio, together with other colleagues active in neutrino physics, was awarded the Breakthrough Prize for Physics for the studies that led to the discovery of neutrino oscillations. He is currently a member of various Italian educational and cultural institutions and is a Research Professor at the University of Chicago, where he continues his research on neutrino physics.